Blueprint for Success

NAWIC Celebrates its First 50 Years

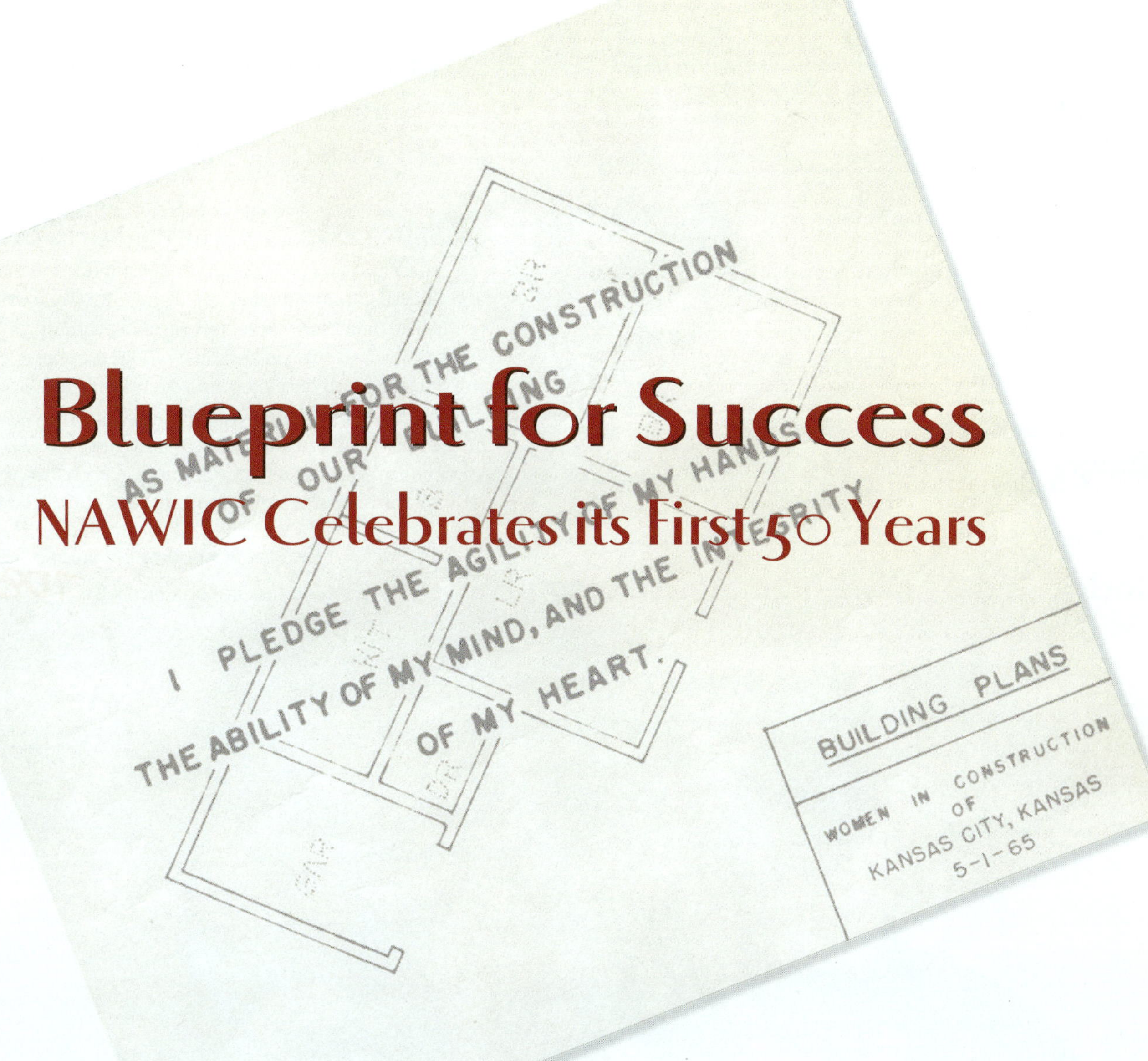

NAWIC's Core Purpose:
"To enhance the success of women in the construction industry"

Index

M.T.

M.T. Publishing Company, Inc.
P.O. Box 6802 • Evansville, Indiana 47719-6802
www.mtpublishing.com
Graphic Designer: Thalita A. Floyd-Wingerter

Author: Nancy Lybarger

Editors:
Kara D. Roberson
Misty D. Overman

Library of Congress Control Number: 2005922545
ISBN: 1-932439-22-6

Printed in the United States of America.

Introduction

Rosie the Riveter was there when her nation needed her. And women in construction continue to be solid building blocks of their society through their professions and service to their communities and the world.

When the National Association of Women in Construction gained its national charter in 1955, the United States was coming out of the Korean Conflict; the Baby Boom was on; the housing market was skyrocketing; automatic washers had been introduced; cars were big and thirsty; aluminum and plastic were used in kitchen tables and chairs; few women were doctors or engineers; and most mothers stayed home with their children. Women did not face the wide choice of careers that are available to young women of the 21st century. Albert Einstein died; Disneyland opened in California; and Jonas Salk's polio vaccine was declared safe. Bill Haley's *Rock Around the Clock* was released.

What hadn't happened: microwave ovens, wireless communication, personal computers, NASA, or 9/11. Bread was less than 25 cents a loaf, and nobody had even thought of Star Wars (the movie or the weapon) or the Beatles. Apple and blackberry meant fruit, not personal computers and hand-held electronic devices. Rap was not a music genre.

What had happened: WWII and the Korean Conflict, and veterans returning from both had GI Bill benefits to invest in education and housing. The construction market boomed along with the post war economy.

In 1955, it was practically unheard of for a woman to work in the construction industry, much less own a company involved in construction. Women have come a long way in construction in the last 50 years.

In 2003, women made up nearly 10 percent of the construction industry, according to the Bureau of Labor Statistics (BLS) *Current Population Survey*.

Within the industry, here's how the numbers break down, according to the BLS report:

- At 549,000 employees, sales and office workers are the majority of women in construction, with 56.3 percent;
- Managers and professionals were at 23.2 percent, with 226,000 women;
- Production and transportation employees at 1.3 percent, with 13,000.

Between 1995 and 2003, the number of women in construction increased 18 percent, from 762,000 to 975,000.

In 1953, when 16 women in Fort Worth, Texas, wanted to form a group that would support women in the construction industry, they couldn't have dreamed what that organization would look like today. In the beginning, *Women In Construction* (WIC) of Ft. Worth was a social group. Members met for tea or dinner, wearing proper hats and gloves.

They held fundraisers to support worthy causes. They sponsored dinners for their bosses. They knew their area of the construction business from the inside out: their specialty was "Girl Friday."

Two years later, the group became the National Association of Women in Construction (NAWIC). And in just a few years, the dainty hats and lacy gloves disappeared.

Women in construction were wearing hard hats and pagers and carrying clip boards as engineers, architects, estimators and construction managers. Women were moving into the construction industry in larger numbers. They still knew their end of the construction industry from the inside out, but they were making their way from the reception desk to the board room.

They needed training and certification. Today, there are 5,800 women in the organization, with 184 chapters. In its 50 years, NAWIC has advanced the causes of all women in construction whose careers range from business owners and office managers, to tradeswomen. Members have moved from meeting for tea parties to meeting their counterparts across the world; from getting together for game nights, to gathering to build houses for other women.

Barbara Alleman, NAWIC president 1994-1995, said one challenge she faced when first getting started was expanding the role of women in construction.

"Although the Association was initially formed as a friendship group, education, networking and promoting the advancement of women in construction later became the focus of NAWIC. These challenges were addressed by developing continuing education programs for members, and forming the scholarship foundation to attract and assist students to seek careers in the construction industry," she said.

NAWIC has developed educational opportunities for members and their communities. For children, the Block-Kids and other design competitions bring the world of construction to life – and hopefully arouse their interest in construction as a career. Members can take advantage of courses designed to help them prepare for certification examinations.

Since its founding, the NAWIC Founders' Scholarship Foundation and NAWIC chapters have awarded more than $4 million in scholarships to students in construction-related majors.

NAWIC has developed the Crystal Vision and Crystal Achievement awards to recognize the achievements of women in construction, as well as those who support women in the industry. The national campaign for Women in Construction Week is held the first full week of March annually and provides opportunities to recognize women in construction and to educate the public about their jobs and the industry.

The organization grew from those first 16 women to a national organization that encompasses most of the United States, one Canadian province, and, most recently, it spread to sister organizations in South Africa, the United Kingdom, New Zealand and Australia. Gone are the teas, but there are still Regional Forums and the Annual Convention where old friends meet, new friends are introduced, information is shared about the industry, and the sisterhood continues. It will be interesting to watch the next 50 years in NAWIC unfold.

Presidents

2004-2005	Nancy A. Eaton, CCA, CIT	Grapevine, Texas	1978-1979	Donna L. Meidling, CIT	Houston, Texas
2003-2004	Luci H. Roberts, CCA, CIT	New York, New York	1977-1978	Marcella Curry*	Boston, Massachusetts
2002-2003	Linda A. Litle	Salt Lake City, Utah	1976-1977	Patricia M. Pridmore	San Francisco, Calif.
2001-2002	Marcia Rackley	Nashville, Tennessee	1975-1976	Mary Ann Nall	Philadelphia, Penn.
2000-2001	Cindy J. Crawley, CIT	Anchorage, Alaska	1974-1975	June N. Barton	Denver, Colorado
1999-2000	Denise Norberg-Johnson, CCA	Reno, Nevada	1973-1974	Eva S. Poling	New Orleans, La.
1998-1999	Patsy M. Smith	Anaheim, California	1972-1973	Janith J. Gould	St. Louis, Missouri
1997-1998	Mary Ellen Ledbetter	Atlanta, Georgia	1971-1972	Bonnie M. Granger	Portland, Oregon
1996-1997	Evelyn P. Clark, CCA	New Orleans, La.	1970-1971	Marie M. Marshall	Atlanta, Georgia
1995-1996	Susan Levy, CCA	Washington, D.C.	1969-1970	Margaret Borg*	San Antonio, Texas
1994-1995	Barbara Alleman, CCA	Denver, Colorado	1968-1969	Florence Hawisher*	Honolulu, Hawaii
1993-1994	Margaret L. Eure	Chicago, Illinois	1967-1968	Grace W. Dollens*	Washington, D.C.
1992-1993	Jane F. Williams, CCA	Dallas, Texas	1966-1967	Dorothy O'Connor*	Chicago, Illinois
1991-1992	Joan Mehos	Orlando, Florida	1965-1966	Nelda Weatherly*	Miami Beach, Florida
1990-1991	Darline H. Johnson	Nashville, Tennessee	1964-1965	Martha Knowles*	San Diego, California
1989-1990	Carol C. Ericson	Minneapolis, Minn.	1963-1964	Letti Nixon	Memphis, Tennessee
1988-1989	Judith T. Short, CCA	Seattle, Washington	1962-1963	Florence Creighton	Atlanta, Georgia
1987-1988	Joyce A. Lemons	Toronto, Ont., Canada	1961-1962	Clara Wilkerson Tuck*	Oklahoma City, Okla.
1986-1987	Sandra B. Glassie	Reno, Nevada	1960-1961	Lois J. Acker*	New Orleans, La.
1985-1986	Jean J. Morrow	Little Rock, Arkansas	1959-1960	Carrie Ann Marquette*	Amarillo, Texas
1984-1985	Marilyn J. Camin	New York, New York	1958-1959	Lucille Holman	Baton Rouge, La.
1983-1984	Mary A. Magee	Louisville, Kentucky	1957-1958	Faye Brown	Houston, Texas
1982-1983	Kathryn B. Pate	Kansas City, Missouri	1956-1957	Peggy Whistler*	Dallas, Texas
1981-1982	Jan L. Burger	Albuquerque, N.M.	1955-1956	Doris Efird*	Fort Worth, Texas
1980-1981	Lura W. Bates, CCA	Honolulu, Hawaii			
1979-1980	Arlean L. McPherson	Phoenix, Arizona			

Town indicates the location of that term's national convention.

Founding members of Women in Construction of Fort Worth, Texas.

NATIONAL ASSOCIATION OF WOMEN IN CONSTRUCTION

National Headquarters

Founding members were honored at the NAWIC Executive Office ribbon cutting ceremony. From left were Ethel McKinney, Alice Ashley, Sue Bowling, Margaret Cleveland and Doris Efird.

Below: National Association of Women in Construction headquarters, Fort Worth, Texas.

Inset: The cornerstone of the Executive Office honors the architect-engineer company that designed the building in 1983, and the general contractor, James Conlee, Inc.

In 1957, Faye Brown first proposed establishing a National Executive Office. A committee was appointed a decade later.

In 1970, the Association approved setting up shop in Washington, D.C., with the services of Association Management, Inc.

Two years later, the Association approved the move back home to Fort Worth, Texas. Jack T. Holmes & Associates (later changed to McKone & Co.), a public relations and management firm, was the support services provider.

In 1980, NAWIC established its office in the Morrow Building before the 1983 purchase of the building at 327 South Adams Street for the NAWIC Office. Kathryn B. Pate was NAWIC President at the time.

Ironically, one of NAWIC's founding members, Nina Ruth Jenkins, worked for the company in charge of building NAWIC headquarters.

NAWIC National Office Ribbon Cutting Ceremony, 1983.

In order to qualify as a charter member, women must have worked in the construction industry for five years and had to attend the charter presentation. Charter night was September 11, 1953, at the Carvey Dining Room. Ninety-six women were present, but only 34 qualified as charter members.

When she described the founders of the organization, Alice Ashley said, "We were women with electricity in our veins, cement dust on our shoes, sawdust on our minds…busy, busy, busy, filthy things."

The first year they were together, members of Women in Construction of Fort Worth raised more than $2,700 and donated it to the Foundation for Visually Handicapped Children. Ironically, Ashley would eventually lose her sight to retinitis pigmentosa.

Not long after WIC started, women outside Fort Worth began to express interest in joining. In order to allow that, the charter was rewritten, and the group became the National Association of Women in Construction (NAWIC) on May 17, 1955.

Highlights

The women who chartered Women in Construction of Fort Worth, founded September 11, 1953, were actively employed in the construction industry and had been doing business with each other for years; but few personally knew each other. When they did get together, they decided to form the organization for support and fellowship. They were networking before it became fashionable.

Founding members were Alice Ashley, Ida May Bagby, Carolyn Balcomb, Jimmie Blazier, Sue Bowling, Margaret Bubar, Margaret Cleveland, Era Dunn, Doris Efird, Ronda Farrell, Hazel Floyd, Nina Ruth Jenkins, Ethel McKinney, Irene Moates, Mildred Tarter and Edna Mae Tucker.

Right: Founding members (left to right): Alice Ashley, Sue Bowling and Irene Moates.

Members celebrate at an early gathering.

The Fort Smith, Ark., Chapter was chartered July 26, 1958. Two national officers presented the charter. From left in the back row were Margaret Holden, treasurer; Mary Gibson, vice president; and Alice Maledon, secretary. In the front row, from left, were Ida May Bagby, NAWIC extension director; Newrany Lambert, chapter president; and Faye Brown, national president.

The nonprofit organization held its first National Convention in Fort Worth, July 14, 1956. The first slate of national officers was elected. Doris Efird, Ida May Bagby, Gladys Thomas and Margaret Cleveland were respectively named president, vice president, secretary and treasurer.

The following year, Dallas hosted the gathering, followed by Houston and Baton Rouge, La., in subsequent years. In 1955, Dallas was the second chapter chartered, followed by Houston in 1956, Corpus Christi and Amarillo in 1957, Odessa, Lubbock and Baton Rouge in 1958. Records show that in the first four years, NAWIC had grown to 500 members.

By 1959, NAWIC boasted 28 chapters in eight states. That year at the National Convention in Baton Rouge, La., three chapters tied for the extension award. Dallas, Fort Worth and Memphis shared the honor.

As the Association grew, six regions were established. Regional forums were held beginning in 1960 to keep members informed about NAWIC happenings, offer workshops and educational opportunities and fun times together. As a result of the redistricting of Region 1 in 1991, Region 14 was established. As of 2005, there are 184 chapters in the United States and Canada. Each region has a director elected for a two-year term.

Six charter members attended the 25th Anniversary Forum: Ethel McKinney, Nina Ruth Jenkins, Doris Efird, Era Dunn, Margaret Cleveland and Alice Ashley.

The cause of NAWIC remains the same as when those first women joined together: *to enhance the success of women in the construction industry.* More formally, NAWIC's objectives are:

• To unite for the mutual benefit of the women who are actively engaged in the various phases of the construction industry;

• To promote cooperation, fellowship and a better understanding among members of the association;

• To promote education and contribute to the betterment of the construction industry;

• To encourage women to pursue and establish careers in the construction industry;

• To provide members an awareness of the legislative process and legislation as it relates to the construction industry.

The core values of the organization are still as crucial as when they were adopted: **Believe in ourselves as women; persevere with the strength of our convictions; and dare to move into new horizons.**

Left: Fort Worth Chapter members help celebrate the chartering of the Houston, Texas, chapter.

Above: Alice Ashley.

Alice Ashley

Pauline L. Lesch, Fort Worth, shared her thoughts about some of the founding members. "It was a pleasure to get that phone call each month from Alice Ashley …'This is Alice Ashley, and I'm your Call Girl,' she would say."

Not only did Alice take reservations for monthly meetings, "she would tell me who the speaker was, update me on what was happening in the lives of fellow chapter members, and pump me for information about members, their companies, and anything of interest going on in the industry."

She was a walking encyclopedia of the construction industry.

"Once when I paid her a visit," Lesch continued, "she showed me how a legally blind woman could make phone calls – big cards with big names and phone numbers handwritten on them. And I think a great memory helped, too."

Alice was the office manager of Anderson Engineering in Fort Worth for many years. When she was elected the first president of WIC, she had been in the industry for two decades.

Going blind was a challenge for Ashley. Her husband had deserted her when the disease was discovered. As her sight failed, she had to take up a cane to help her navigate. She named the cane Jezebel.

Doris Efird

When Pauline Lesch was chapter president-elect, she shared a room with Doris Efird at the 1992 National Convention in Orlando, Fla.

"She had arrived early for meetings with the national past presidents and Association leadership, so she was all settled in the room when I arrived," Lesch said. "As soon as I walked in the door, she threw open her special suitcase and announced that no one traveling with Doris Efird ever went hungry. There, I saw a carefully packed case of canned meats, crackers, cheese, fruit, nuts and other snacks."

Lesch was amazed at how Doris "fluttered around that convention." She seemed to know everybody, and everybody knew her. "They not only knew her, they revered her. It was like traveling with the Pope," Lesch said.

Before the formal banquet at the end of the Convention, Efird asked Lesch what she was going to wear. "When I showed her my simple two-piece suit, she said, 'Why, we're about the same size. Next time, you must come to my house and pick out a dress.' I didn't realize Doris was the absolute queen of sequined gowns," Pauline said. "She looked gorgeous at the banquet, but then again, Doris exuded an inner beauty that didn't depend on glitz or glitter."

Efird was honored for her service to NAWIC at a reception in Fort Worth on the 44th anniversary of the national charter presentation.

Efird served as the first national president, while remaining an active member of the Fort Worth Chapter until she passed away in 2001. "During her four decades of service to NAWIC, Efird logged in thousands of volunteer hours to a cause she believed in, one echoed in the original mission statement: to promote and support the advancement and employment of women in the construction industry."

An *Image* article written in 1999 spoke of Efird's love and labor for the organization. One example cited was that two years before her death, she decided the association needed a video documentary about its founding. She helped raise the funds needed for the project, located the production company, wrote the script and served as the video's narrator. The video is available for purchase through the NAWIC Store.

Ida May Bagby

Faye Brown, NAWIC president 1957-1958, remembered Ida May Bagby as a woman who lived, ate and breathed WIC – "even fed WIC to her family.

"Some 30 or more years ago, a very scared (Can you imagine her ever being scared?) and timid sort of young mother of four children showed up at the offices of James T. Taylor and Son, General Contractor, to help them out of a tight spot by agreeing to work on a temporary job," Brown recalled.

That temporary job lasted many years. When she retired and was ready to file for Social Security, Taylor called her to "come back and get the company back in the construction business."

In 1956, Brown asked her to be the NAWIC National Extension Chair. "Almost every weekend, Ida May was on the road with two or three of the Fort Worth girls, visiting nearby towns to sell WIC. Sell it, she did!"

Brown called Bagby, *Mrs. WIC,* and said, "No other WIC anywhere in the United States has done as much for our organization as Ida May."

Ida May was the keeper of "stuff" for the organization. When the NAWIC library was established at headquarters, it was named for Bagby. She delivered

(continued on page 16)

Right: Ida May Bagby.

The library at NAWIC headquarters was named in honor of founding member and early historian Ida May Bagby.

NAWIC Founders. Standing, from left, are Margaret Cleveland, Ethel Kickler, Doris Efird, Nina Ruth Jenkins, Margaret Bubar and Ida May Bagby. Seated, from left, are Sue Bowling, Irene Moates and Alice Ashley.

Early Officers. From left, bottom row, are Doris Efird, president; Linda Farrell, vice president; Louise Abnot, secretary; Trace Chase, treasurer. From left in the back row are Alice Ashley, Imogene Pardue, Nina Ruth Jenkins, Peggy Whistler and Margaret Cleveland, all board members.

Doris Efird, right, and Margaret Cleveland, center, received Life Membership plaques from NAWIC, presented by Marie Marshall, for their service to the Association.

The Oklahoma City, Okla., Chapter was chartered July 18, 1959. Presenting the charter was Martha Knowles. Chapter President Margaret Tuttle received the charter. At the right is Ida May Bagby, NAWIC Extension Director.

Right: Five Fort Worth Chapter members and ten prospective Dallas Chapter members met to discuss plans for organizing the Dallas Chapter on March 22, 1955. Officers of the Dallas Chapter were M. Lee Dillon, president; Evelyn Harrison, vice president; Janis Wright, secretary; and Bobbie Kent, treasurer.

At the 1979 National NAWIC Convention, from left, were Arlean McPherson, President-Elect; Marcella Curry, Immediate Past-President; Donna L. Meidling, President; and Eva S. Poling, Past President.

NAWIC

ADOPT
A
HIGHWAY
NATIONAL ASSOCIATION
OF WOMEN
IN CONSTRUCTION

Susan Levy, past national president, helps move boxes at the 1996 NAWIC Convention in Washington, D.C.

most of the material to the library from her home. For years, if anyone needed to know anything about the organization's history, Bagby was the woman who most likely could find the information.

She was responsible for many of the scrapbooks that detail the early history of the Association. The scrapbooks are filled with photographs and mementos of chapters' activities and officers, greetings and congratulatory notes, telegrams and cards. Early scrapbooks contain invitations to friendship teas, bosses' annual dinners, and articles from newspapers and construction magazines that detail the young Association's activities.

Although friendship and sisterhood are priorities of the Association, looking at later scrapbooks, the reader can see NAWIC has left the social club aspect and has moved toward education and employment support.

Irene Moates

The first secretary-treasurer of Fort Worth's WIC was Irene Moates. She also served as the second president of the group. She was employed as the office manager for Roden Construction.

"Why, I'm the odds-and-ends person in charge of all the gruesome details," she said in an article in *Fort Worth Magazine* in 1955.

Actually, she was in charge of completing bids, cost estimates, cost details, payroll, bookkeeping and correspondence. In the process of doing all those tasks, she learned to read blueprints, structure bids and other intricate details of construction.

"No job's too tough, nor hours too long for the seasoned woman in construction," she said in the article.

Faye Brown

Brown was gracious enough to share the anecdotes about her sister WICs. An article was published January 9, 1958, in the *Fort Worth Press* detail her election as national president and told much about her opinion of women in construction.

She had a shortwave radio in her office to communicate with employees in the field. Being a short wave set, it picked up conversations all along the bandwidth.

One day, she heard it crackle and then heard a man hailing his office, saying he could not deliver an oil shipment to a construction site because a mean dog would not let him in the gate. The man was in Cleveland, according to Brown.

His office manager reminded him to pay attention to the notes she had written for him. "If you had read your chart, you would know to call him 'Sam,' and he won't hurt you. Don't, and he'll tear your leg off."

Brown told the *Press* that her duties took her to Louisiana, California, North Carolina, Connecticut, Oklahoma and all around Texas, and everybody who knew her was worried about her getting to appointed meetings. She admitted she was infamous for running out of gas, to the point that her husband, Guy, threatened to take away her car keys if it happened again.

A husband in this century would not consider that! A 21st century woman would just purchase roadside assistance as insurance, and pay the cell phone bill.

NAWIC Past President, Sandy Glassie, shared this anecdote with Pam Dullum:

Before the Association's headquarters became known as the NAWIC Office, it was called the NAWIC Executive Office, or NEO.

"We used to hire a service to tape record our NAWIC Board of Directors' meetings, and we would receive a transcript along with the tapes," Glassie said.

Getting the NAWIC story out to the public, the Danville, Ill., Chapter built this float for various parades.

When she was Board Secretary, Glassie received a copy of a meeting transcript and read through it. There were more than a few items assigned to "Annie O."

"While I recognize that none of our Directors or Officers believe they have accents, they might," Glassie said. "It seems we had a lot of Southerners on the Board that year. The (apparently) Yankee transcription service converted NEO (spoken in Southern drawl) to 'Annie O' but never did quite catch Annie's last name."

Chapter Highlights

Anchorage

The Anchorage, Alaska, Chapter chose the Can-struction Project because it met a critical need in their community to help fill Food Bank of Alaska shelves. It helped that the members possessed a unique set of talents enabling them to construct a project entirely of non-perishable foods.

More than half the chapter members participated in the project, which was directed by Tamie Taylor and Jessica Cederberg, a licensed architect and past chapter president, respectively. Plans were drawn for a giant electric can opener, based on an idea of Evelyn Clark, then-immediate past president for NAWIC.

Taylor and Cederberg met to discuss the building materials required, and like a good construction manager, Taylor told her architect the quantity needed to complete the project. Two weeks before the actual building event, several members met in the shop of Chapter President Chris Jett and constructed a mock-up of the design to verify quantities and assure the structural stability of the project.

Using seven layers, each consisting of 144 cans of soup, the foundation of the can opener measured 3 feet, 8 inches per side. After the seventh layer, the can opener was narrowed at the top to accommodate a knife sharpener on the back. On top, the opening lever was constructed of boxes of crackers.

The final project consisted of 1,188 large cans of soup, 27 boxes of crackers, two round crackers, five pepperoni sticks, a can of tomato paste and a can of tomato sauce.

Chapter members were busy collecting donations for the supplies needed. More than a dozen people participated in the actual building of the structure at the University Center, an Anchorage mall.

After the structure was complete, electricity was wired to the top front of the can opener, and a spinning "disc" was installed to simulate a working can opener. The NAWIC project was the only one in the contest that had moving parts.

Final touches were a tower simulating a can waiting to be opened and a knife (sporting a NAWIC red handle) in the knife sharpener.

The judges presented the chapter's entry two winning ribbons: *Most CAN-Did Use of Creativity* and the *CAN-Do Award*. Mall shoppers gave the entry the *People's Choice Award* as well.

Always thinking about membership extension, chapter members hollowed out a cracker box and filled it with NAWIC and chapter fliers. They received more than half-a-dozen calls inquiring about membership.

Phoenix

The Greater Phoenix, Ariz., Chapter can claim notoriety of the best kind. Charter members of the group didn't know amateurs could publish a professional dictionary, but they did. According to chapter member Mary Duffy, the first *Construction Dictionary* was published on Mother's Day 1966. As of 2005, the chapter was working on its 10th edition.

"All these women were trying to do was print a list of the construction and slang terms heard on job sites for use by the gals back in the office. It has been an unqualified success and a labor of love by many of our members," Duffy said.

Proceeds from the first edition were donated to NAWIC's Founders' Scholarship Foundation, and subsequent editions have provided funds to help purchase NAWIC's national headquarters building in Fort Worth and support Operation Woman Power, which evolved into the NAWIC Education Foundation. When the student chapter of AGC at Arizona State University assisted with the expanded third edition, more than $75,000 was contributed to the Del E. Webb School of Construction for a scholarship endowment.

The chapter also built and drove a float in the Fiesta Bowl Parade from the early 1980s through the early 1990s. "Members from all over the country would come to help build the NAWIC float, and the National President of NAWIC each year would be featured on the float," Duffy said. "The exposure on national television was priceless."

In late 2004 when this history was being prepared, one of the charter chapter members, Lodine Robinson, was still active and will be receiving her 40-year pin in March 2005.

Colorado Springs, Colorado

After the first Construction Career Fair – held in Lewisville, Texas, in 1999 and attended by 1,300 students and teachers from

25 schools in 15 districts – was such a success, the idea spread throughout the country.

The Colorado Springs, Colo., Chapter launched its first Construction Career Days event in 2003, working with the State Department of Transportation, FHWA, AGC and the Colorado Construction Association. The event attracted 200 high school students from six districts and more than 70 adult volunteers to direct and help with the activities. Malisa Martinez organized the event for her chapter. She said many hours of planning and organizing preceded the event.

The students "experienced many aspects of the construction industry through exhibits, displays, equipment demonstrations, skill competitions and hands-on activities," Martinez said.

During the day, participating students got to maneuver manlifts, backhoes, mini-excavators and operate a radio-controlled mini compactor. Other students learned how to fit pipe and the correct way to drive nails.

In 2004, the chapter partnered with the Colorado Contractors Association. Along side Career Days, the Colorado Springs Chapter held another career event in Castle Rock, between Colorado Springs and Denver. Chapter President Dodi Walch said it was a two-day event, with students from both areas participating.

Members

Many NAWIC members have taken to heart the challenge to get the word out that women are good at construction careers and that construction careers are good for women.

Nancy Bailey Farrar

On her own since she was 18, Nancy Bailey Farrar was tired of dead end jobs, and at the urging of her then-boyfriend, she took a welding class. She was the only woman in a class of sixteen, and she loved the program.

"I've always enjoyed working with my hands, and I seemed to pick up the trade easily," she said.

She worked on a number of projects, including heavy equipment, structural steel and bridges. She worked for two general contractors before she started her own business, Nancy's Welding, in 1981. She had to keep her second job as a cocktail waitress in order to make ends meet.

Nancy's mother died in 1980. A few short months later, Nancy was diagnosed with cervical cancer and had a radical hysterectomy. She was determined and returned to work. She also continued welding school and obtained her boiler's license in pipe welding.

To build her business, she concentrated on upgrading equipment and constructing garages. As one of only a handful of women welders in Maine, she earned quite a reputation. She now travels the state, basically working out of her truck.

"Being a woman has been a real boost to my business," she said. "Companies always remember me and the good work I do because I am a woman."

But she faced another bout with cancer in 1997, with Hodgkin's Lymphoma. After months of treatments, she conquered the illness. She said she learned a more important lesson about her relationships with men.

"…For the first time in my life, I realized just how short life is and was determined to never stay in another relationship that wasn't right for me," she said, in an *Image* article about ending an 11-year, unhappy relationship.

In 1998, while working another construction job, she met her future husband, David, a crane operator. They were married in July 1999.

"…My life is perfect with David. We share all the same interests. We have Harley Davidsons, snowmobiles, enjoy camping and even get to work together on the same job sometimes. I'm so glad I found the right person," she said.

Vera Rappazzo

Working in a man's industry is one of the most difficult challenges women face, according to Vera Rappazzo, a member

A Certificate of Appreciation for CONSTRUCTION INNOVATOR 2004-2005 was presented to National Association of Women in Construction for its outstanding support of the goals and concerns of subcontractors in the Los Angeles/Orange County by the American Subcontractors Association, Los Angeles/Orange County Chapter at ASA's Awards Banquet, October 21, 2004. There to accept the award on behalf of NAWIC are, from left: Robbin Loomis, President, Pomona Chapter; Norma Shearer, President, San Gabriel Chapter; Marlene Hargrove, Immed. Past President, Pomona Chapter; Krista Wilkie-Boswell, Region 12 Director; Ruth Worden, Pomona Chapter; Mary Ellen Ledbetter, Past NAWIC President, President, Ventura-Oxnard Chapter; Delores Whelchel, Pomona Chapter; Madeline Chapman, Orange County Chapter. Also in attendance, but not pictured was Sharon Bangs, Past National Secretary and San Gabriel Chapter member.

of the Capital District (Albany, N.Y.) Chapter. She retired in 2000, after 45 years of working in the family's business, Rappazzo Electric.

"People in this business have always been hesitant to accept women, especially in the trades. I wanted to show them we could do it," Rappazzo said.

She and her husband, Charlie, started a bakery in the early 1950s, but Charlie's first love was electrical engineering. So, they closed the bakery and opened an electrical contracting business. At first, they worked out of their kitchen and then moved the office into the basement of their home. Eventually, they bought some land and built an office.

Before she retired, she worked at almost every level of the family's business – as a bookkeeper, bidding jobs, working on bonding and insurance proposals, secretary, office manager and company president – all while raising a son and two daughters.

Rappazzo and her husband worked for commercial buildings and hospitals – even installing the first MRI machine in Albany. Later, they installed traffic lights with the State of New York.

Rappazzo credits her membership in NAWIC as part of her success as a woman in construction.

"Being in NAWIC has been great. We (members) bond together. The industry as a whole is starting to become more and more accepting of women working in these fields. We have proven ourselves and shown that we can do it, too," she said.

She was recognized in the summer of 2000 as one of the *100 Women of Excellence in the Capital District of New York*.

Pam Dullum

While she was in the Navy's Civil Engineer Corps, Pam Dullum, PE, CCA, learned what it's like to be a woman in a male-dominated society. One of her first duty stations was on the island of Diego Garcia, in the middle of the Indian Ocean. She was one of only 300 women of the 3,000 people on the island.

Dullum never let her gender hinder her dreams. All through school, Dullum was a whiz at math, and in high school, she discovered physics. A teacher recommended mechanical engineering, but her uncle steered her to civil engineering.

She attended college on a Naval ROTC scholarship, so she knew what her first job would be after graduation. It turned out to be a 12-year job, where she was a project manager for the Naval Facilities Engineering Command. Her projects included the construction of 500 housing units and a submarine escape trainer.

"I learned the differences between management and the folks who get the work done," she told *The NAWIC Image* for a November/December 1999 article. "I also learned teamwork and a great deal about taking an idea and turning it into a reality through planning, programming and budgeting."

After the Navy, Dullum worked for Raytheon Systems Company, which handles contracts for the Federal Aviation Administration (FAA). She has a master's degree in civil engineering and earned her engineer's license and CCA certification.

Among her accomplishments at Denver International Airport with Raytheon was managing the first project to be completed on time and within budget. She worked as a resident engineer for a 6,500-square-foot childcare center, the Terminal Doppler Weather Radar and the FAA Terminal Radar Approach Control Facility. She was promoted to engineering manager, where she supervised 20 designers and engineers.

As of 2005, Pam works in Phoenix, Ariz., at Gervasio & Assoc., Inc. as a forensic engineer, investigating complaints and claims regarding problems and failures in civil engineering and construction. "The breadth and level of my experience got me this job. I guess all those strange assignments along the way paid off," she said.

While working with the Navy and Raytheon, Dullum moved around a lot. However, she's always been close to a NAWIC chapter. She said NAWIC "has been a lifeline," serving as a source of networking, friendships and involvement. Since she joined the Association in 1985, she's been in seven chapters. She has belonged to the Norwich-New London, Conn.; Danville, Ill.; Ventura-Oxnard, Calif.; Metro Denver, Colo.; Salt Lake City, Utah; Tacoma, Wash.; and Greater Phoenix, Ariz. Chapter. She's probably been in more chapters than any other member, by calculation of the people at National Headquarters who know those things.

"I try to stay in touch with all of them. Of course, in NAWIC, you are never out of touch," Pam said.

She has served on the National Strategic Plan Committee. She believes NAWIC plays an important role and serves as a resource mentoring young people in the construction industry.

Since she has found civil engineering such a rewarding profession, she would like to see more women join her. It's rewarding, challenging and gives one a sense of accomplishment. "…And the compensation is not too shabby," she said.

Janis Gail Reek

In her quest to help women in the construction industry, one NAWIC member has traveled to war-torn Kosovo to offer assistance. Janis (Jan) Gail Reek agreed to a two-week consulting assignment in Pristina, Kosovo, with CHF International, a U.S.-based organization focusing on community development in low-income areas and places in transition. She previously had worked on a three-week venture to South Africa for CHF International.

In Pristina, she was to work with a group of women in construction to explore forming a professional organization similar to NAWIC. The 15 women were so excited about it, they formed Fortesa – Femrat ne Ndertim (Fortress Women in Construction) before Reek left the country. She said they borrowed heavily from the NAWIC organizational manual.

"I helped the women to choose a mission and set goals for their organization; identify key issues; develop a set of bylaws; and select leadership," Reek said.

Kosovo was ravaged by a civil war in the late 1990s and was receiving international assistance in 2002 when Reek visited. She said the women's primary goal is to make a living.

"The women want to be able to compete successfully for contracts. Just like us, they want to know their affiliation with a professional organization will lead to better prospects in business.

"High customs duties on the import of raw materials and the import and export of finished goods is the key issue affecting construction businesses in Kosovo. Fortesa members chose this issue as the topic for their first regular meeting held in June (2002)," Reek said.

Deb Naybor – Sisterhood in Construction

After a trip to South Africa to speak to her sisters in construction down there, Deb Naybor became inspired to help African women build themselves better lives. She had met Ingrid Verwey, founder of the South African Women in Construction organization at the 1999 NAWIC National Convention. The two realized they had much in common and were working toward some of the same goals.

"In 2000, I traveled to Johannesburg, South Africa, to attend the Annual SAWiC Meeting and speak on empowerment and women in nontraditional fields. Little did I know that the role of women in construction *is* traditional in the Zulu tribe, where women had woven homes from grasses for centuries, while the men tended herds of livestock," Naybor recalled.

She said she learned much while touring job sites and talking to SAWiC members about their jobs and their lives. She was amazed that many of the women lived in tin shacks and earned less than $2,000 a year.

She became good friends with three women – Thandi, Violet and Sarah – and vowed to help SAWiC members any way possible. She returned home to New York and quickly collected tools and safety wear to help her three friends get better jobs. Equipment like that is not provided by South African employers.

Months later after returning from other travels, Naybor discovered Sarah's box had been returned. It wasn't until she returned to South Africa in 2001 that she learned Sarah had been stoned to death because she reported domestic violence.

"Her SAWiC sisters sat at her bedside watching her die and cared for her daughter after she was gone. I knew economic stability was the solution to being able to leave a dangerous situation and vowed to help poor women to be able to choose to leave a violent home life," Naybor said.

She praised NAWIC chapters for answering her calls to help poor women around the world. "Over the past four years, NAWIC members raised funds to buy a brick-making machine for a poor village in Malawi…They collected donations and built the first-ever secondary school in that village, allowing 100 kids (80 orphans, with no chance without a free school) to get an education that was not possible before.

"Other chapters have bought hand-powered sewing machines to start a sewing cooperative in Uganda in a village where the average family earns $400 a year. Regional efforts have collected thousands of yards of fabric to provide materials for job creation…and the postage money to ship it overseas," Naybor said.

She is currently the executive director for *Both Your Hands*, a nonprofit organization that connects caring communities for global self-sufficiency. She owns a land surveying firm in Alden, N.Y., and belongs to the Buffalo, N.Y., Chapter.

In January 2004, Mama Debi's House opened in a Malawi village. She's acted as a clearing house for thousands of donations, from construction tools and supplies to more than 3,000 yards of fabric to supply sewing cooperatives in Uganda, Senegal and on U.S. Indian reservations. Clothing and medical supplies have been shipped to several villages.

"I raised the funds to bring South African women in construction trades to the United States for training in business, safety and construction skills.

"In 2002, I visited a small village in Uganda and brought a women's group a personal donation of $250. The group voted to create $25 microloans to buy goats or pigs.

"Within 12 months, all 37 women in the group had borrowed and repaid the loans, and more than half had doubled the income of their families," Naybor said.

With the award money from her national 2004 Business Optimist Award, Naybor established *Both Your Hands* as a nonprofit agency. She also set up a program for community groups to adopt a poor village for as little as $250.

At the end of 2004, Naybor reported, along with the microloan program in Senegal, *Both Your Hands* is building a medical clinic in Uganda; training South African women in construction skills; and training youth in leadership. Quilting cooperatives are being established on U.S. Indian reservations; orphanages in Malawi are being supported, and leaking school roofs repaired; funds are being collected to build a hospital in Sri Lanka; and microloan programs are scheduled for Mexico and India. University students are raising money to build an outhouse at a Senegal school, and middle school students in New York raised $400 in pennies to buy school lunches for kids in Uganda.

"*Both Your Hands* teaches that no amount is too small," she said. To this point, Naybor has been able to complete projects without grants or large corporate donations.

Naybor operates a $1 million-annually land surveying business in upstate New York and is enrolled in an online graduate program. She travels the world speaking about *Both Your Hands* and spends many hours in the United States talking to students about life in African villages, encouraging them to get involved in creating change.

"This just shows what one person can do when she is determined and committed to her goals," said Ramona L. Gallagher of Buffalo, N.Y. "Debbie is truly a selfless person who inspires others to get on the bandwagon and support her efforts to make positive differences in the lives of women and children around the world."

Naybor received the 1998 Crystal Vision Award.

Dee Engel

Each year, many NAWIC chapters and members participate in Habitat for Humanity projects. The organization was founded by Millard and Linda Fuller in 1976. For many years, President Jimmy Carter and his wife Rosalynn have been Habitat's most visible supporters.

In July 1994, NAWIC member Dee Engel traveled 438 miles from Minneapolis, Minn., to Eagle Butte, S.D., to help with a Jimmy Carter Work Project for Habitat. The Carters and the Fullers were among the 1,500 volunteers participating in the building blitz for Lakota Sioux Indians who live on the Cheyenne River Indian Reservation. Volunteers ranged in age from 18 to more than 70 years, and according to Engel, more than one-third were women.

At the time, Engel was in her second term as president of the Minneapolis/St. Paul Chapter and in her twelfth year of NAWIC.

"By the time we arrived (the first morning at the work site), the majority of the lumber had been cut, and the trusses had been made by the homeowners since they must contribute 500 work hours to Habitat projects," Engel said.

She worked with fellow Dow volunteers on a house that would eventually belong to Ila Sand and her five children. Engel works as a construction product sales representative for Edward Sales, who markets the Styro-foam brand insulation that Dow Chemicals donated to the blitz and to all the 1994 and 1995 Habitat projects.

"I started out building the exterior walls in the morning, and by the afternoon, I was installing Styrofoam™ sheathing. This was a new experience for me, as most of my carpentry work had been limited to roofing and working on sheetrock."

From Tuesday to Thursday of the construction blitz, Engel said she helped secure wiring in the walls and nailed siding to the house. Winds kicked up as they were siding the house, making it a little more complicated than usual. Engel said she had to chase after a couple of siding pieces.

"I was reminded that Eagle Butte got its name from the migrating bald eagles that were attracted to those winds. The birds, like the siding, it seemed, could soar endlessly," she said.

Friday, the house was completed and the Sand family was given the keys and moved in about 4:30 p.m.

Ruby Poat

The first president of the Memphis, Tenn., Chapter was Ruby Poat. She was a manager for the Memphis Builders' Exchange, a clearing house for exchange members working in the various arms of the construction industry. Ruby said the Exchange provided messaging and secretarial services for members. Prospective clients and suppliers could call the Exchange and leave messages for members, like a physicians' answering service. Ruby passed along the information to members.

With the advent of answering machines and cellular phones, such a service isn't much needed anymore, but it helped a lot of people keep up with business in the first half of the 20th century.

The amazing thing about Ruby was that she was nearly 70 years old when she helped establish the Memphis chapter and took on the job of president for the charter year.

In 1960, the Memphis chapter raised more than $40,000 to build a new wing in a home for handicapped children, Happy Acres.

Kathryn Pate

Past National President (1983-84) Kathryn Pate was the poster child for how women can succeed in the construction business. She was featured in a September 21, 1983, *Kansas City Times* article.

Pate established Overland Steel, Inc. in North Kansas City in 1956. She started at the company as a secretary when she found herself a divorced mother of four children in need of income.

A decade later, the owner announced he was closing the facility. Pate then led the effort to convince employees to pool their funds and take over the business.

The emphasis of her term focused on professional growth in construction and membership opportunities.

Katherine Pate with Ronald Reagan.

Margaret Borg

Margaret Borg, past national president (1969-70), is credited with establishing the NAWIC national office in Washington, D.C., and launching the publication of *The NAWIC Image*, the official magazine for the Association.

But that's not all Margaret Borg did in her lifetime. In a 1988 *Intermountain Contractor* magazine article, Borg described her accidental career in construction. In 1946, she took a part time job as a secretary while she was working on a journalism degree. She retired from the Intermountain Chapter of the National Electrical Contractors Association as executive manager 42 years later.

In 1964, Borg was one of the first women in Utah to get involved in NAWIC. She served as NAWIC secretary, where she conceived the idea of a national headquarters for the Association.

"It was quite a challenge in those days because the Association had no executive office, no central place where information could be distributed," she said.

After her stint as president, Borg chaired the NAWIC long-range planning committee and began the process of establishing the Association's national headquarters back home again in Fort Worth.

She was elected a Fellow of the Academy of Electrical Contracting in 1989, the first woman in that role.

Scholarship Foundation

Not long after the Association formed, members began to worry about getting more women involved in the construction industry and in NAWIC. In order for women to work their way up the corporate construction ladder, they needed more education. To attract top notch students to the construction industry, the scholarship foundation was instituted. Lois Acker, 1961 NAWIC president, is credited with the idea for a scholarship program. A scholarship committee was named in 1962, and a trust was proposed. Scholarships would be awarded to National Merit Scholar Finalists pursuing careers in the construction industry.

In 1970, the Founders' Scholarship Foundation was established by combining the foundation's general fund, the Lois Acker Award and the Phoenix (Arizona) Endowment Scholarship. The $200,000 goal was achieved in seven years. Marie Marshall was named the first administrator to serve a five-year term, 1974-1979.

In 1977, the trust agreement was amended to extend scholarships to students who were not National Merit finalists and to reduce the administrator's term to three years. Scholarship applications are currently available at NAWIC Online.

NAWIC Education Foundation

In the late 1960s, the Bureau of Labor Statistics started predicting a shortage of labor in the construction sector by the late 20th century. Qualified help would be hard to find.

Former NAWIC President Darline Johnson told the 1981 national meeting, "Forty-two percent of new hires will be women in the 1990s…Never before has there been such a prime opportunity for women to enter the construction industry."

Even before that, the women of NAWIC realized an opportunity to get women into a job sector previously dominated by men. The NAWIC Education Foundation (NEF) was formed to provide the resources needed for women who wanted to earn certifications in their fields.

In 1971, the Association established the Introduction to Construction training program and the Certified Construction Associate (CCA). The NAWIC Education Foundation went to work to underwrite the programs.

The CCA course is a comprehensive self-study program open to anyone who wants to advance into a management or administrative position in the construction industry. It's a six-part course developed for NAWIC by Clemson University. When students complete the program, they take an exam for certification.

Also available to NAWIC members is an introduction to construction course covering industry basics.

In 1972, the degree and special courses were established and continued until 1991. Intermediate Construction courses began in 1981. An apprenticeship training program began in 1982, and NEF joined the American Council for Construction Education (ACCE).

The Construction Industry Technician (CIT) program was established in 1993. The Construction Document Specialist (CDS) program, based on NEF's Intermediate Construction textbook, began in 1998.

Mary Ellen Ledbetter, office manager for Apex General Contractors of Ventura, Calif., and NAWIC president 1997-1998, said the most valuable seminars NAWIC offers are the introduction and intermediate construction classes.

"For someone just starting to work in the construction industry, these are vital," she said.

NEF was designated to administer the Block-Kids annual program within the K-12 Industry Enhancement Program. Career Days and the CAD/Design/Drafting contest were also placed under the NEF umbrella. In the late 1990s, the Building Design Program for middle school and junior high students was instituted. In 1998, the *Build It* video was introduced to schools to familiarize children to the construction industry and encourage them to explore construction careers.

The Block-Kids program has received rave reviews from educators and increasing support and involvement from the construction industry. The program was the brainchild of Carol Ericson when she was president-elect in 1988.

"I was searching for an idea for a new challenge during my year as President," Ericson said.

She received a call from Erma Lamousin, a friend of hers in Biloxi, Miss., who wanted to know of anybody connected with LEGO®, headquartered in Hartford, Conn.

Ericson did not have any connections or know anyone at LEGO®, but her curiosity was aroused. Lamousin said her boss's wife was doing a church project and was looking for a donation or a deal from LEGO® to use in a *Building Blocks for the Church* program.

"While we were talking, the idea that something like this would be a great construction project for NAWIC came to my mind," Ericson said.

She gave the idea much thought and then asked Lamousin to chair the NAWIC Construction Industry project.

"I told her it would be launched during the 1989 Convention, but we needed to work on guidelines. …The guidelines were not making enough headway to meet our deadline, so I asked Susan Levy to help out. She really took off with it and helped with a generous donation, as well," Ericson said.

Not every region participated the first year, she recalled, but it caught on in no time. "I'm glad to say that it makes me happy and proud to have been responsible for such a successful program," she said.

The contest was introduced at the Convention with a skit written and produced by JoAnn Strano. Ericson also announced a contest in which all the Regions were asked to "name" the Block-Kids.

Regions that hosted contests were to send photos of the winning projects to Ericson for final judging. Cash prizes were awarded to the top three projects.

"They were sent to me (I had not planned this part out), so I had a local general contractor, an engineer and an architect help choose the winning entries with me," Ericson said.

Members of the Wilmington, Dela., Chapter built two mascots for their Block-Kids program: *Connie Struction* and *Bill Ditt* in 1995. Susan Chaffee chaired the project, which received high praise.

"The group of women in the local NAWIC organization are committed to the education of students about careers in the construction industry…We appreciate this commitment to the education process. The day was an excellent way of exposing our students to the variety of careers to which they might aspire," the school principal wrote to the newspaper after the event.

The article in *The NAWIC Image* in June 1995 noted that once volunteers judge the contest, they want to do it again, and once the word about the contest got out in the community, the construction industry got behind the chapter, offering financial support, prizes and locations to hold future contests.

The concept of the program is to give contestants each 100 blocks, some string, poster board, a rock and aluminum foil and see what they can build. Judges have been astounded at the creativity and ingenuity of the youngsters who participate. The children targeted by this program are in grades 1-6.

The Building Design program not only introduces middle school students to aspects of construction, it also emphasizes team work. The teacher uses 10 prepared lesson plans, and students solve design problems. Teams design floor plans and build a scale model of their project. Oral presentations complete the project. The pilot for this NEF program was launched in the fall of 1997. It was not designed as a competition.

The CAD/Design/Drafting competitions have been held in all 14 regions. They are targeted at high school students who are enrolled in design and drafting classes.

Expansion

Everyone in the construction industry knows bricks and mortar are only one aspect of the business. Regardless of their position in the industry, the women who founded NAWIC knew about building bridges among their sisters in construction. The bridges are designed to support women in different fields, and most recently, to support women in countries around the world.

From its beginning in Fort Worth in 1955, NAWIC has gained international affiliates in four countries and helped establish the Association in Canada and the Netherlands. NAWIC's scope and influence have spread to other countries as well. Members have traveled for the Association to China, Kosovo and South Africa to advance the core purpose of the organization: *To enhance the success of women in the construction industry.*

When SAWiC founder Ingrid Verwey visited the 1999 NAWIC Annual Meeting, she told the Association, "I am not talking to 800 strangers, but to 800 friends, who made me feel not only welcome, but a part of you…"

The international affiliation agreement signed between the two Associations was the third for NAWIC.

Australia and NAWIC signed NAWIC's first agreement in 1995. NAWIC-Australia was founded by Paula Gerber-Jones. In 1996-1997, the Job Exchange program was established with Australia. Carol Brubaker and Tracey Clavell, both members of the NAWIC-Australia association, were the first to participate.

In 2004, NAWIC-Australia held its first National Convention in Sydney.

Gerber-Jones, then a senior associate in the Melbourne Office of the international law firm of Mallesons Stephen Jaques, spent her first four years with NAWIC in the Greater Santa Monica, Calif., Chapter.

Three years after the first agreement was inked, New Zealand became a NAWIC affiliate, launching on its own with assistance from NAWIC sisters in Australia.

The fourth affiliation agreement was signed with the United Kingdom in 2003 at NAWIC's 48th Annual Meeting in Salt Lake City, Utah. Members from the United Kingdom organized in 2002. By its first anniversary, the UK association had five regional groups.

Emma Keyte, said one of their goals is "to raise the number of young women entering the industry. We want girls to aspire to the 'glamour' of becoming architects, engineers, construction lawyers or project managers the same way that many currently aspire to be actors, filmmakers, musicians or models."

Keyte said while networking is important to the group, *change* is one of the key objectives. She said the members are determined to achieve equality in the construction industry.

In 2001, Verwey visited NAWIC national headquarters to gather information so SAWiC could start organizing provincial chapters and improve the structure of the national office in Johannesburg. South African women have benefited from the SAWiC initiative, Verwey said, to empower women to access contracts, training and finance and networks in the construction industry.

While on a 1998 business trip to the United States, Verwey met with several NAWIC members from North and South Carolina.

This was followed by information and assistance from NAWIC officers and staff and eventually led to the affiliation agreement.

In 2004, with help from NAWIC contributions and support from Buffalo, N.Y., author and NAWIC member

Left and Below: Members of South African Women in Construction were honored at the 2004 NAWIC convention in New York City.

Members of the South African Women in Construction at the NAWIC convention, New York City, 2004.

that NAWIC has established associations in the United Kingdom, Australia, New Zealand and South Africa. Bagby was the first Fort Worth WIC extension director, appointed by Faye Brown in 1956. She then served as NAWIC extension chair for many years.

The International Affiliate Agreement was signed with South African Women in Construction (SAWiC) on September 3, 1999. Past NAWIC President Patsy M. Smith and SAWiC founder and president Ingrid Verwey inked the agreement during NAWIC's Convention.

It pledges the full support of NAWIC to its sister Association, providing for a free exchange of programs, materials and expertise to advance women in the construction industry.

Deb Naybor and 20 SAWiC board members came to New York City for the Annual Meeting.

The Netherlands Chapter is no longer active. Currently, only one Canadian chapter in Ontario is active in the Association.

Not only has NAWIC expanded around the globe to help women in the construction industry, but since 1992, the Association has opened its doors to corporate sponsorship. Five levels of corporate sponsorship are available.

With corporate support, NAWIC can step up its efforts to promote construction education and industry awareness.

Those partnerships have expanded to other construction associations, universities and major manufacturers of construction materials.

Verwey founded SAWiC in 1997, following the passage of the South African constitution and Equity Act, which requires that women be employed in all sectors of the economy. SAWiC's mission is to empower women to gain access to contracts, training, financing and networks in the construction industry.

Extension

If Ida May Bagby was still alive, she would be ecstatic that NAWIC has grown to encompass most of the United States and a couple of Canadian provinces. Even more, she'd be thrilled

International Affiliates

Australia	1996
New Zealand	1998
SAWiC	1999
United Kingdom	2003

Partnering agreements

By the late 1980s, Department of Labor (DOL) warnings triggered alarms throughout the construction industry with its statement that by the millennium, there would be a serious worker shortage. The door was opening for women who knew of the opportunity and possessed the qualifications for many of the jobs that would be available.

The Education Foundation expanded class offerings. NAWIC participated in career fairs to entice women into the industry. Scholarships were extended to students who planned careers in the industry.

Also, between 1993 and 2003, NAWIC signed 17 partnering agreements and memoranda of understanding with construction associations, government agencies and business groups, according to an article in the *NAWIC Image* magazine. Altogether, more than 30 associations work with NAWIC to share resources, safety training and problem resolutions.

In 1993, an agreement was signed partnering the Association with the U.S. Army Corps of Engineers. Also in 1993, the Association and a major industry player, the Associated Builders & Contractors, agreed to partner, pledging to share resources and programs to further mutual goals.

In 1994, NAWIC and the DOL signed a partnering agreement, which would include the Women's Bureau, Bureau of Apprenticeship and Training, Job Corps, OSHA (Office of Construction and Engineering), Office of Small Business and Minority Affairs and the Glass Ceiling Commission (now defunct).

The DOL agencies agreed to cooperate in outreach activities aimed at women's employment, training and business opportunities in the construction industry; to coordinate efforts to identify women in the skilled trades who could serve as role models for young women in the Job Corps trade programs and provide publicity for success stories about Job Corps graduates who enter the industry. Also, the agencies agreed to coordinate efforts to develop job placement opportunities in the skilled trades for qualified female Job Corps graduates; update NAWIC with relevant changes to construction regulations and procedures; and inform contractors and subcontractors that NAWIC is a recruitment source for women in the construction industry.

NAWIC and the National Center for Construction Education and Research (NCCER) signed a joint resolution in 1997. The NCCER pledged to increase the number of women in construction by implementing educational resources.

The construction industry's heftiest heavyweight, the Associated General Contractors of America (AGC), and NAWIC joined forces in a partnering agreement in 1998. Both associations committed to work toward enhancing the image of the construction industry.

Also in 1998, NAWIC signed a partnering agreement with the Women's Business Enterprise National Council (WBENC). Since then, WBENC has implemented a national certification process, whereby women business owners are accepted by 500 major corporations, getting a foot in the door to bid on contracts, etc.

In 1999, a partnering agreement was signed with the American Subcontractors Association, and a memorandum of understanding with the U.S. Small Business Administration was drawn up to provide women entrepreneurs opportunities and training.

Perhaps the most visible of all the partnering agreements signed by NAWIC is that with Habitat for Humanity International's Women Build department in 2000. Many NAWIC chapters have participated in building projects with Habitat, but oddly enough, Habitat had not seriously encouraged women to volunteer for projects. By agreeing to cooperate more closely, Women Build can tap the collective power of women to accomplish its goal of completing 100,000 new homes by 2006.

Also signed in 2000 were agreements with the Construction Financial Management Association, the American Institute of Constructors and the Southern Building Code Congress.

Agreements were signed with the American Society of Professional Estimators, the National Society of Professional Engineers and the NAWIC Education Foundation in 2002.

The Federal Highway Administration, the Surety Association of America and the American Road & Transportation Builders Association signed partnering agreements with NAWIC in 2003.

In 2004, NAWIC signed partnering pacts with both Women Work! The National Network for Women's Employment and the Society for Marketing Professional Services.

"Through the agreements, NAWIC hopes to create avenues to promote, educate and support women," according to a news release.

Women Work! and NAWIC hope to further advocacy, education and networking between both organizations. They will exchange ideas, materials and resources to train and educate women seeking careers in the construction industry.

NAWIC chapters have taken the cue from national and have developed partnerships in their areas. For example, in partnership with Women Build, NAWIC chapters are involved in Habitat projects all around the United States. In 2003, the Memphis, Tenn., Chapter joined a Women Build project. Members did everything from framing the house and laying roof shingles to cutting and hanging siding. Those who couldn't be there supported the effort with financial contributions.

The Block-Kids program has connected NAWIC chapters to many other organizations by using members to judge annual contests, support the program and provide a location for the contestants to build their projects.

Chapters are networking with NAWIC's partnering organizations. For example, the St. Louis, Mo., Chapter holds a yearly joint meeting with the American Society of Professional Estimators, the American Association of Cost Engineers and the Professional Management Institute. The San Bernadino-Riverside, Calif., Chapter works with other construction associations to present an annual mini-trade show and dinner. The members of the associations get to network and stay up-to-date on construction industry issues.

The Pittsburgh, Penn., Chapter jointly sponsors a construction-related activity during the Downtown Street Fair. The chapter is looking for other city-wide events to take its booth where members can spread the word about the Block-Kids program and construction industry career opportunities.

For several years, the Anchorage, Alaska, AGC Chapter has hired the local NAWIC chapter to plan and operate its annual meeting. The NAWIC members coordinate registration, fill packets and mail information about the meeting, among other things.

Many chapters have become closely involved with the Associated Builders and Contractors and the Associated General Contractors of America since those partnering agreements were signed.

"Perhaps more than anything, the partnership between NAWIC, ABC and AGC have helped educate men about the enormous benefits of women in construction and how they can be an important resource in addressing the trade worker shortage…The partnerships have made it possible for the two organizations to tap into the resources of an overlooked sector of the work force: women," according to a *NAWIC Image* article in 2003.

Several chapters have participated in the Federal Highway Administration (FHWA) Career Days. Construction Career Days are held in more that 20 states.

Partnering also opens doors of opportunity to interact with members of other organizations, such as providing educational seminars at chapter meetings.

Along with the agreement with the American Society of Professional Estimators came the opportunity for NAWIC members to take the Association's courses at "members only" prices.

Past NAWIC president Luci H. Roberts, CCA, CIT, 2003-2004, said in an article that the emphasis during her term in office was to encourage members to use the partnering agreements.

Besides the tangible benefits of partnering, Roberts said she was striving to "pursue new avenues where NAWIC can be recognized as an equal among our counterparts in the industry."

Challenges

During her year leading NAWIC, past president (1999-2000) Denise Norberg-Johnson, CCA, said the biggest challenge faced by women in construction is getting into policy-making positions at work. She made it her goal that year to help members *Break the Glass.*

"That means opening the pretty glass cases in which we have looked decorative but have played little part in policy making. And it means that we, as women, will accept the challenges offered to us, and in fact, demand the right to those challenges; that we will risk a few cuts to step through the glass we break and breathe the fresh air of the big world outside," Norberg-Johnson said.

She warned construction industry 'good ole boys' to open the doors or get out of the way.

"We have the tools," she said. "Now we want to work on the projects, and show you what we can do. We'll either work for you, or we'll compete against you."

As NAWIC enters its second fifty years, there are several challenges facing the Association, its members and the construction industry. The Association, along with many other organizations, faces the challenges of recruiting and retaining members. Younger members expect more return on their dues and time investment.

Generational shifts in the officers, board, members and staff will change the culture of the Association. Younger members have different perceptions and loyalties to the organization. They have different preferences for programs and services. Their volunteer involvement may be less than their older sisters because they have many more options for volunteering and more pull on their time.

Because there are fewer young people, there will be fewer potential members in the pool of possibilities. As well, that is the greatest challenge ahead for the construction industry as a whole: qualified people to fill positions.

That is where an association such as NAWIC can provide a valued service to the industry – recruiting young people and making sure women who are entering the work force for the first time, or those who are investigating new careers, know they have training and certification options available.

A 1993 Bureau of Labor Statistics (BLS) report encouragingly said that the construction industry is the fastest growing sector for women business owners. The BLS, however, is forecasting a serious shortage of qualified labor for the construction industry as older workers retire.

NAWIC studies predicted in 1990 that the construction industry would need 270,000 new employees every year, and a report by the U.S. Census Bureau indicated 42 percent of the new hires would be women. Women currently comprise about ten percent of the construction work force.

Several NAWIC members were surveyed for this book. One of the questions was, "What do you perceive as the greatest challenges the Association faces in the future?"

Evelyn Van Dyke, former Region 7 Director, said she thinks the current challenge is to meet the needs of all members that are being bombarded with distractions from a multitude of sources, including families, business and careers.

"Meeting this diversified demand within the time frame members allocate to NAWIC requires drastic changes in how NAWIC functions on both the national and chapter level," she said.

Past NAWIC president Evelyn Clark agreed with Van Dyke about attracting Generation Xers and Yers into the Association.

"Our Traditionalists and Boomers are aging and burning out, and younger women aren't as likely to spend the time or money to join a women-only group," Clark said.

Pauline McIntosh, CCA, CIT, former Region 10 Director, said the Association membership has become so widely diverse throughout the construction industry that it is difficult to offer programs of interest to everyone.

McIntosh noted that women in construction trades are still fighting discrimination on the job.

"They come up against the 'good ole boy' network and some of them are fighting to hold their jobs," she said.

Three task forces were appointed in 2000 to address the challenges – Membership, Governance and International – by then-president Cindy Crawley, CIT. She said task force members would evaluate the steps necessary to attract and keep younger members.

"NAWIC has a rich history of supporting and advancing women in construction. If we want the Association to build on its rich history for a long time to come, we need to sow the seeds of our future today."

Shelves Trade Book

Construction industry students at Westark Community College will have a new reference book, a dictionary of trade terms given by Fort Smith Women in Construction. Public library cardholders may also use the Westark bookshelves. From left are Max Burns, director of learning resources; Verna Day, new president of the local construction women, and Betty Jones, outgoing president.

NAWIC Chapter Histories

NATIONAL ASSOCIATION OF
WOMEN IN CONSTRUCTION

Fort Worth, Texas
Chapter #1, Region 7
Charter Date: September 11, 1953

The Fort Worth, Texas, Chapter originally began as Women in Construction of Fort Worth, founded on September 11, 1953, by 16 women who were looking for a support system. The founding members were Alice Ashley, Ida May Bagby, Carolyn Balcomb, Jimmie Blazier, Sue Bowling, Margaret Bubar, Margaret Cleveland, Era Dunn, Doris Efird, Ronda Farrell, Hazel Floyd, Nina Ruth Jenkins, Ethel McKinney, Irene Moates, Mildred Tarter and Edna Mae Tucker. This progressive group of women had the foresight to create an atmosphere where they could network and support each other professionally and personally. Their forward-thinking helped make this chapter and this Association what it is today.

Dallas, Texas
Chapter #2, Region 7
Charter Date: August 23, 1955

2005 marks the 50th anniversary of the Dallas Chapter. The chapter was chartered in August of 1955 with 35 chartering members, four of whom went on to be chapter presidents. The chartering president was M. Lee Dillon. The first organizational meeting was held March 22, 1955. Later, dues were set at $5 a year. National dues were $2. The first Board meeting was held April 19, 1955, at which time the Secretary, Janis Wright, was instructed to write a letter to the Fort Worth Chapter requesting that Dallas be chartered as the second chapter of Women In Construction. The first official membership meeting was May 2, 1955.

Houston, Texas
Chapter #3, Region 7
Charter Date: June 21, 1956

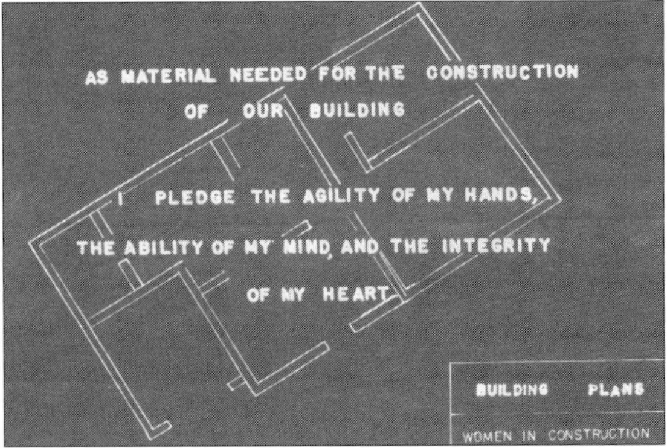

The owner of Gregory Edwards, a Houston HVAC contractor, encouraged his female employees to attend a meeting for women in the construction industry. The first organizational meeting of what was to become the Houston Chapter was held in the home of Florence Harrison. In addition to Florence, Grace Dockal, Patsy Minor, Frances Galvin, Carrie Ann Marquette, Jane Harris, Ouida Rouse and Ann Judice attended this meeting. These eight ladies called their friends, and 44 women signed the charter to establish the Houston chapter on June 21, 1956. Of these 44 charter members, Grace Dockal and Laura Feagin still retain their memberships.

Corpus Christi, Texas
Chapter #4, Region 7
Charter Date: April 26, 1957

The Corpus Christi Chapter was chartered on April 26, 1957. Through the years, we have had many members serve at both the regional and national levels. National committee appointments, directors and even a national president have been developed from within our own chapter ranks. We also have many members with CCA and CIT certifications. We have held Block-Kids and CAD contests and have built playgrounds and houses. It has been said the members of our chapter know how to work hard, play hard and, whenever possible, do both at the same time. Here's to another 50 years!

Baton Rouge, Louisiana
Chapter #6, Region 5
Charter Date: February 8, 1958

The Baton Rouge Chapter was chartered on February 8, 1958, with 14 members. Our sponsoring chapter was the Houston, Texas, Chapter, and we were the first chapter chartered outside of Texas. Although the Baton Rouge Chapter was not chartered until February 8, 1958, the Fourth National Convention was held in Baton Rouge in 1959. Baton Rouge presented the first scholarship award in 1962, ahead of any other chapter. For our community service project in 1968, we purchased a leopard for the Baton Rouge Zoo. After 46 years, the Baton Rouge Chapter is still going strong.

Fort Smith, Arkansas
Chapter #10, Region 5
Charter Date: July 26, 1958

The Fort Smith Chapter was chartered on July 26, 1958. It was the first chapter in the state of Arkansas and tenth chapter in the United States.

Austin, Texas
Chapter #7, Region 7
Charter Date: February 15, 1958

The Austin Chapter was chartered on February 15, 1958, with the assistance of the Dallas Chapter. Notable Dates: January 1966—Groundbreaking Ceremony for Gazebo; July 1, 1968—Gazebo Dedicated; 1971—Established the Florence Barnes Memorial Scholarship (later changed to the Barnes-Davis Scholarship); 1997—First NAWIC member, Carol Brubaker, participated in the International Job Exchange Program with Australia; 1997—Tracey Clavell, first NAWIC Australian member, participated in the International Job Exchange Program; 2001-2002–First Austin Chapter member, Luci H. Roberts, CCA, CIT, elected as national president for 2003-2004.

San Antonio, Texas
Chapter #11, Region 7
Charter Date: August 9, 1958

During 1957 and 1958, several San Antonio women, acquainted by telephone, decided to meet and have dinner and get to know each other better. They were all working in male-dominated occupations in the construction industry. They understood they would benefit from a network of women with whom to share information and ideas. The first meeting was a success, and they soon began meeting monthly. They called their group "Women in Construction." They heard about the ladies in Fort Worth who were organizing women employed in the construction industry into chapters for a new association. The San Antonio women became the eleventh chapter of NAWIC on August 9, 1958.

Gr. Little Rock, Arkansas
Chapter #12, Region 5
Charter Date: August 16, 1958

The Gr. Little Rock Chapter was chartered on August 16, 1958. Today, we still have one active charter member. An accomplished chapter, we have produced three national presidents and eight Region 5 directors. Our membership first surpassed 100 members in 1980, and in 1986, we hosted the Annual Convention with near-record attendance. Instrumental in the development and implementation of the NEF programs, we have made education a priority through our continued support of the Foundation and NFSF. From our grand beginning to an even greater future, we promise to continue the legacy of furthering the advancement of all women in construction.

Memphis, Tennessee
Chapter #13, Region 5
Charter Date: August 16, 1958

The Memphis Chapter's records were destroyed many years ago. One of our members, Joyce Gregory, obtained a copy of our charter from National when the Convention was in Dallas. It is dated August 16, 1958, and is signed by 25 members. She was told it was very nice and held at the Peabody. Ruby Poat is listed as the chartering president with Ruth King as vice president. Memphis was said to have had its paperwork in first, but Little Rock was closer. So, the chartering group from National went to Little Rock Chapter 12 on Friday and then came to Memphis Chapter 13 on Saturday. This is the story of why Memphis and Little Rock have always had a special bond as sisters chapters.

Waco, Texas
Chapter #14, Region 7
Charter Date: September 6, 1958

The Waco Chapter was chartered on September 6, 1958. We meet the second Tuesday of each month at the AGC Office. Martha Knowles, Past National President from the Dallas Chapter, was instrumental in getting the Waco Chapter started. She and Shirley Brown would come to Waco every year and install our officers. She did this until her health failed. Past National President Luci H. Roberts, CCA, CIT, has been installing our officers ever since.

Boston, Massachusetts
Chapter #15, Region 14
Charter Date: August 25, 1958

The Boston Chapter was chartered on August 25, 1958, by Gloria Salvo, our first chapter president. Gloria started the Boston chapter with 18 other women after she read about NAWIC in *The Boston Globe*. The Boston Chapter has sponsored the following chapters: No. 1 of Rhode Island; The Granite State, N.H.; Greater Worcester, Mass.; Toronto, Ontario, Canada; Greater Springfield, Mass.; and Southeastern Massachusetts. Boston has had many distinguished leaders, including Mary Johnson, past president. She remains active in the Boston Chapter. Boston sponsors joint meetings with ASHRAE, as well as panel discussions at BuildBoston every year. Boston also awards scholarships annually to deserving students.

Nashville, Tennessee
Chapter #16, Region 2
Charter Date: January 31, 1959

The Nashville Chapter was chartered on January 31, 1959. There were 32 women who first made the commitment to organize this chapter. We hosted the 2002 Annual Convention and five Regional Forums. We currently have eight active members who have served as chapter president. They include Donna Lamb (current President 2004-2005), Dottie Brown, Betty Capps, Betsy Lynn Harrington, Michelle (Hobby) Thomas, Susan Moon, Susan Carson and Patsy Smith, who also served as the 1998-1999 national president.

New Orleans, Louisiana
Chapter #17, Region 5
Charter Date: January 25, 1959

In 2004, the chapter celebrated its 45th Anniversary. Our charter president, Rita Fiegenschue, is still an active member. In 1959, Rita chartered the chapter with 29 members. The original focus was based on friendship with other women in the industry. As women's roles in the industry have expanded, the chapter's focus moved toward educational programs. NAWIC has played a vital role in our members' success in achieving business goals. Our members have made an impact on local and national levels. Gypsy Prinz was a national parliamentarian, and Barbara Alleman has served as the national president.

San Francisco, California
Chapter #19, Region 10
Charter Date: April 18, 1959

Marie McDonald, a still active founding chapter member, took the lead in having our chapter chartered. Marie and Helen McIntosh traveled around the San Francisco Bay Area promoting the chapter, which was chartered in April 1959. Her hard work helped build this chapter and other chapters throughout the West. The chapter has always been looked upon as a tenacious group of women. Despite the many career challenges facing women in construction, we strive to create a chapter that embodies the core purpose of NAWIC, supports our local communities and educates the younger generation. The diversity within our chapter is a reflection of the uniqueness of the city we call home.

Shreveport-Bossier, Louisiana
Chapter #20, Region 5
Charter Date: May 16, 1959

San Diego, California
Chapter #21, Region 12
Charter Date: April 30, 1959

The San Diego Chapter was chartered on April 30, 1959. Since its founding, the chapter has worked toward the betterment of women in the construction industry. Throughout the years, San Diego has actively worked to provide networking and education opportunities for its members and to give back to the construction industry and the community. Each year the chapter participates in a variety of events, including WIC Week, Block-Kids and Career/Construction Expos. The chapter also gives back to the community and the construction industry by awarding two annual scholarships.

Oklahoma City, Oklahoma
Chapter #25, Region 7
Charter Date: July 18, 1959

The chapter was organized on June 11, 1959, and chartered on July 18, 1959, with 22 members. Margaret Tuttle was the first president of the chapter. At the September 1993 National Convention, Oklahoma City Chapter member Pearl Jones received a Red Rose Recruiter Award. She was the first to receive this award from Region 7. In September 1997, the Oklahoma City Chapter participated in the first-ever Women Build Habitat for Humanity House in Oklahoma.

Jackson, Mississippi
Chapter #28, Region 5
Charter Date: August 8, 1959

The Jackson Chapter was chartered on August 8, 1959, with 38 members. In the past 45 years, Jackson has had three Region 5 directors, two national secretaries, two national vice presidents, one national president-elect and one national president. Lura W. Bates is still a very active member of the chapter; in the past 45 years, she has served in all of these roles. We look forward to another 45 years!

Greater East Bay, California
Chapter #30, Region 10
Charter Date: January 15, 1960

We began as the "Oakland" Chapter in 1960. We became the "Greater Alameda County" Chapter, but we are now the "Greater East Bay" Chapter. We are thrilled to have charter member Faye McCann and thirty-year-plus member Rosemary Buell to link us with our chapter's past. Flea markets, barn dances, Block-Kids, scholarships and Girl Scout Ms. Fix-It Badge Days have been popular fund raisers and community events over the years. In 2000, we celebrated the chapter's 40th anniversary with a gala attended by many friends of NAWIC, past and present members, and Oakland city officials. Here's to our 45th and NAWIC's 50th!

Pine Bluff, Arkansas
Chapter #31, Region 5
Charter Date: January 16, 1960

Early officers of the Pine Bluff, Ark., Chapter.

Indianapolis, Indiana
Chapter #34, Region 4
Charter Date: May 21, 1960

On May 21, 1960, the Indianapolis Chapter received its charter. The Dallas, Texas, Chapter was the sponsoring chapter. The Indianapolis Chapter has organized several chapters. Many chapter members have served as national officers, directors and on national committees. Indianapolis has hosted numerous Region 4 Forums, APCs, mid-winter conferences, summer conferences and one Tri-Regional Conference. Two of our members were able to travel with a delegation to China and bring back ideas about construction outside the United States. We've participated in Women Build Habitat projects and have performed several other community service projects throughout the years.

Tampa, Florida
Chapter #36, Region 3
Charter Date: June 8, 1960

The Tampa Chapter chartered on June 8, 1960, with 18 members. One chartering member, Francene Grivna, is still active. She is currently chapter president and is a candidate for regional director. The chapter's focus is on education – educating our members and future members through Block-Kids and CAD, and awarding scholarships to those interested in pursuing a construction career. Each month, we work with the Center for Women making repairs for needy seniors in our area. Twice, we've participated in the Lymphoma and Leukemia walkathon. We are hosting Region 3 Forum aboard a cruise ship in May 2005.

St. Louis, Missouri
Chapter #38, Region 6
Charter Date: June 25, 1960

The St. Louis Chapter proudly celebrates 45 years of service to the construction industry. We are dedicated to the education of our members and the future work force. We take pride in presenting a professional forum for women and promoting careers in this industry. Highlights – 1962, Charter member Florence Creighton elected NAWIC President; 1972, First Scholarship Golf Tournament; 1989, Work Force Awards to tradespeople, totaling $25,000; 1989, Block-Kids Building Program, National Winners 1989 & 2000; 1994, CAD/Design/Drafting Contest, National Winners 1997, 2001, 2002 & 2003; 2001, Building Design Program; 2003, Construction Visionary and Member-of-the-Year Awards, Scholarships totaling $300,000.

Chattanooga, Tennessee
Chapter #40, Region 2
Charter Date: August 13, 1960

The Chattanooga Chapter was established in 1960. Our first president was Judy O'Neal. We have had a tremendous response to our Block-Kids program. We intend to continue, and maybe expand, this program. We also want to continue to develop our relationship with Girls, Inc. This picture was taken at Hardy Elementary School during a weeklong "Design Girl" enrichment program. Two of our members, Judy Grammer and Janet Phillips (back row of the picture) and also Terri Jeter-McAvoy, worked with the girls to develop a zoo design problem and then held a Block-Kids competition for the afternoon session.

Miami, Florida
Chapter #41, Region 3
Charter Date: January 28, 1961

The Miami, Fla., Chapter received its charter January 28, 1961. Eleanor McDonald was our first president, and the chapter started with 13 members. We've been growing ever since. We are empowering the next generation with our ongoing support of a local student chapter. Our chapter has held major networking events, as shown in the photo. Pictured is current chapter president Margaret Danao with our speaker, Denise Mincy Mills. Current officers include, Margaret Danao, President; Rhonda Wimberly, Vice President; Marilyn Mills, Treasurer; and Candace Harris, Secretary. NAWIC Miami Chapter 41 is rocking and rolling.

Los Angeles, California
Chapter #42, Region 12
Charter Date: March 25, 1961

Members of the Los Angeles, Calif., Chapter.

South Bend/Mishawaka, Indiana
Chapter #44, Region 4
Charter Date: April 28, 1961

In 1961, the South Bend/Mishawaka Chapter was chartered by 39 members with a common goal: to expand the role of women in construction.

Our history includes many "WIC Week" activities, such as annual professional seminars, 13 "Block-Kids" programs, four "Dirt and Skirts" events, visiting countless local jobsites, four Habitat for Humanity's "WomenBuild" houses, and building a National award-winning house for Santa for the local downtown mercantile area.

Our numbers have swelled and dwindled many times, but we are determined to remain an active force in the South Bend/Mishawaka construction community!

Pensacola, Florida
Chapter #46, Region 3
Charter Date: May 25, 1961

Quad Cities/Moline, Illinois
Chapter #50, Region 13
Charter Date: August 5, 1961

Lorraine Wright hosted 15 women on May 16, 1961, to organize women in construction. A charter was presented August 5, 1961, with 26 original members. During 1962, 24 new members were inducted. In 1963, Wright was selected as Region 4 Director. Later, we were reassigned to Region 6, and in 1975, we were assigned to Region 13. In 1964, Quad Cities tied for first place in the region for scrapbook, placed third for bulletin and third for speech library. In the late '60s, the Lorraine Wright Construction Awards were introduced honoring owners, architects, and contractors and promoting pride and recognition within the industry.

Atlanta, Georgia
Chapter #49, Region 2
Charter Date: June 16, 1961

Enhancing the success of women in the construction industry has been the purpose of the Atlanta Chapter since we chartered in 1961. Our members have served as national officers and regional directors. We have awarded more than $30,000 in scholarships to students pursuing construction careers. We serve our community by building playhouses for charity; fixing up homes for the elderly; holding Block-Kids and CAD/Design contests for hundreds of students; and supporting education with our many seminars. Atlanta has chartered numerous chapters. Atlanta celebrates women's achievements in the construction industry with our local visionary awards banquet. Our chapter will accomplish much more before our 50th anniversary.

No. 1 of Rhode Island
Chapter #52, Region 14
Charter Date: July 28, 1961

The chapter was chartered in July of 1961. Each year, a special event is scheduled to mark the date. During the year 2000, the chapter sponsored the Regional Forum in recognition of that anniversary milestone. Previously, the chapter hosted APC on two occasions. One unique aspect of our chapter is that we have a family with members that span three generations. Each of these women has held offices as elected officers, including president. The chapter also has three members that are second generation. Each daughter followed in her mother's footsteps. The chapter's construction industry project once received first place at the national level.

Gr. Birmingham, Alabama
Chapter #53, Region 2
Charter Date: June 17, 1967

The Gr. Birmingham Chapter was chartered on June 17, 1967. We currently have 32 members. The Construction Industry and Community Service Committees have been very successful in providing the members with good quality "work days" to help the industry and community. The Tradeswomen Committee is very active and encourages tradeswomen to participate in NAWIC. We have joint meetings with other associations. Although it's "hard work," we still manage to turn projects into a "fun-filled activity."

Savannah, Georgia
Chapter #56, Region 2
Charter Date: August 19, 1961

The Savannah Chapter was chartered on August 19, 1961. We are fortunate to have two charter members, Wauwese Turner and Mamie Lake, still active in our chapter. Our two charter members are a valuable resource in retaining our chapter history. Our Chapter's events each year are the Annual BOSS/WIC Party (to honor our employers), Anniversary Party, Christmas Party and Oyster Roast. We have participated in Habitat for Humanity, Christmas in April, Safe Shelter and Fresh Air Home at Tybee Island. Over the years, our chapter members have enjoyed attending Regional Forums and National Conventions.

Portland, Oregon
Chapter #54, Region 9
Charter Date: August 11, 1961

Sponsored by the Dallas, Texas, Chapter, NAWIC's first northwest chapter was chartered 43 years ago on August 11, 1961, with 31 members. It was originally called "Pacific Region." Our chartering president, Rosalie Hayward, is still an active member, and she has not missed a monthly meeting since 1961. Our highest membership was in 1974 with 86 members. Original dues were $20 plus initiation fee, which included $2 national dues. The chartering dinner was $3.50. As with everything else, our costs have increased over time. The chapter has distributed close to $72,000 in scholarships. We have participated in or contributed to various community service projects.

Fort Wayne, Indiana
Chapter #59, Region 4
Charter Date: November 4, 1961

The Fort Wayne Chapter was chartered on November 4, 1961. NAWIC President, Clara Wilkerson Tuck from Little Rock, Ark., presented the charter. Over the years, the chapter has been active with fund raisers, community benefits, style shows, Block-Kids and CAD. The chapter celebrated its 40th Anniversary in November 2001. We have hosted several Forums and Planning Conferences over the years. The chapter has produced national officers. Arlean McPherson was Region 4 director in 1972, and she went on to become National President in 1979-1980. Diana Miller served as NAWIC Region 4 director from 2000-2002, and the next year she served as NAWIC Secretary.

Puget Sound, Washington
Chapter #60, Region 9
Charter Date: January 13, 1962

The Puget Sound Chapter was chartered in Washington State on January 13, 1962. It was originally referenced as the Seattle Chapter and later became the Puget Sound Chapter. This chapter reaches out to women in the construction industry from Auburn (south-end) to Mill Creek (north-end) to Issaquah (east-end). The chapter has a very diverse group of professionals. Examples include: An owner, designer and permitting coordinator, project/contracts administrator, carpenter, CPA, architect, forensic engineer and more.

Knoxville, Tennessee
Chapter #61, Region 2
Charter Date: July 16, 1966

The Knoxville Chapter chartered July 16, 1966, and will celebrate its 40th Anniversary in 2006. Two charter members, Jean Morrow and Byrd Lunsford, remain active. A third charter member, Vivian Beretta, is no longer active but remains a devoted supporter. The Knoxville Chapter boasts having two members who have been Region 2 Directors. Jean Morrow was Director for 1978-1980 and Angelia J. McNair, CIT is Director for 2004-2006, during NAWIC's 50th Year. Past National President (1985-1986) Jean Morrow is also a Knoxville Chapter Member. Happy 50th Birthday, NAWIC!! We've come a long way baby!!

Sacramento, California
Chapter #63, Region 10
Charter Date: March 24, 1962

The Sacramento Chapter is seated in California's capitol and was chartered on March 24, 1962. Members pictured in this photo are leaning against doghouses built by students at the Sacramento Valley Technical High School (SVTHS). The chapter recently adopted SVTHS as its Community Service Project and serves on the Advisory Board for the SVTHS Construction Pathways curriculum. Member Juanita Kirkpatrick (not pictured) donates her time (courtesy of her employer, Rex Moore Electrical Contractors & Engineers) teaching the students the basics of safety in construction. Members of the Sacramento Chapter are proud to be involved with such a worthwhile endeavor.

Cincinnati, Ohio
Chapter #64, Region 4
Charter Date: April 27, 1962

Cincinnati was the first chapter in the state of Ohio. Two of our charter members are still active today. We salute Julia Gecks and Toni Cinquina for their long commitment to our chapter. Former NAWIC National President, 1988-1989, Judith Short, is also an active member. Judy not only attends meetings regularly but is a sought-after speaker for regional meetings and workshops. We work closely with the SWIC (Student Women in Construction) Chapter at the University of Cincinnati and have initiated steps to form another SWIC chapter at Northern Kentucky University.

Albany, Georgia
Chapter #65, Region 2
Charter Date: April 28, 1962

The Albany Chapter was chartered on April 28, 1962, with 46 charter members. The chapter believes in enhancing the success of women in the construction industry. The members are involved in community projects to improve the construction industry. The chapter organized the Southwest Georgia Construction Training Council, Inc., an apprenticeship program that is still active today. The chapter also provides scholarships to students pursuing an education in the construction industry. For many years, the chapter has participated in various community service projects such as helping visually handicapped children, volunteering at the hospital, buying Christmas gifts for those in need and serving meals.

Tallahassee, Florida
Chapter #72, Region 3
Charter Date: August 25, 1962

The Tallahassee Chapter was chartered on August 25, 1962, with 24 members. This chapter has been supportive of and active in the community as well as regional and national NAWIC functions. Over the years, we've supported the Pace Center for Girls and the Refuge House (through donations and repairs); repaired and refurbished cottages for the homeless; built handicapped ramps, play areas and a rabbit house. In 1999, we were awarded the regional Construction Industry Award for the rabbit house project. We have been actively involved in the CAD and Block-Kids programs. We have 42 members. We are proud to be a part of NAWIC.

Gr. Washington, D.C.
Chapter #67, Region 1
Charter Date: May 18, 1962

The Gr. Washington, D.C., Chapter received its charter on May 18, 1962. The chapter began its first official year with an installation ceremony. Past National President Lois Acker came from Dallas to perform the installation. For more than 40 years, the chapter has continued to champion the advancement of women in the construction industry. The chapter is also involved in encouraging the future generation through Block-Kids competitions, college scholarship funds, Future Force Now and Career Days. One of our past presidents, Eva Poling, went on to serve as national president and is now a lifetime member of NAWIC.

Greater Orlando, Florida
Chapter #73, Region 3
Charter Date: August 24, 1962

The Greater Orlando Chapter was chartered in 1962, as "Orlando/Winter Park," with fifteen women from the local area. We have had many members from the early days become well-respected women in the community and the state, including our own Toni Jennings, the current Lieutenant Governor for the state of Florida. The chapter has members from five surrounding counties. We are a progressive and dynamic chapter. We have assisted in chartering several new chapters close by. We are celebrating NAWIC's 50th birthday this year and look forward to growing with NAWIC!

Las Vegas, Nevada
Chapter #74, Region 12
Charter Date: January 17, 1962

In 1962, Las Vegas was still a very small town, but 31 brave women wanted to be part of this National Association and accepted the invitation to be charter members. Their history in this valley is respected and has changed lives. Always willing to participate, the chapter became known for two main roles: providing education to those in construction and related industries and scholarships to dependents of those employed in construction in Las Vegas. We are proud of our home-grown President, Nancy A. Eaton, CCA, CIT, and look forward to celebrating the continued success of our Association.

Augusta, Georgia
Chapter #75, Region 2
Charter Date: December 1, 1962

The Augusta Chapter was chartered on December 1, 1962. Atlanta was the sponsoring chapter. At present we have no charter members, but Ellen Livingston has been an active member since 1970, having served as president for 12 terms during her 35 years of membership. We presently have only five members but are very active on a chapter level. We sponsored the chartering of two chapters in 1965, Columbia and Greenville, South Carolina. We built a Women Build Habitat House in 1996.

Tulsa, Oklahoma
Chapter #76, Region 7
Charter Date: March 9, 1963

Our chapter has two charter members: Helen McCarty and Blanche Wissabaum. We are proud of Letha Cather, as she was the only region director from our chapter. She is still an active member. When most people think of Oklahoma, they think "Indians." The chartering ladies went to Forums and Conventions wearing Indian outfits.

Eugene, Oregon
Chapter #77, Region 9
Charter Date: April 17, 1963

Chapter member Ellie Cooper is demonstrating the use of equipment to member Carrie Fortier. This was during Eugene's third annual Construction Career Days (CCD). The Eugene Chapter's CCD chair, Stephanie Babb, was so awed by the CCD presentation at the National Convention in Reno, Nev., that she came back supercharged and organized the event. She also chaired it for three years. Our entire chapter has been involved in this event. It has been great to see a high school girl get on a piece of equipment and realize she can do this! CCD is as big a thrill for the Eugene members, as it is for the students.

Gr. Ft. Lauderdale, Florida
Chapter #78, Region 3
Charter Date: April 20, 1963

This chapter was sponsored by the Miami Chapter and chartered on April 20, 1963, with Helenor Mirigliano, president, Joan Alexander, vice president, Lilyan Cappola, secretary and Helen Bard, treasurer. One charter member, Eileen Bolton, and 40-year member Anita Narvaez are still actively involved in the chapter. Member Judy Orr served as national secretary, and Lola Gus, Carol Busby and Judy Orr served as regional directors. Fort Lauderdale has hosted five forums. The chapter has worked with Habitat, supplying materials and labor. The chapter's scholarship fund has awarded scholarships to local college-enrolled students. We are proud of our achievements and dedication to the construction industry.

Evansville, Indiana
Chapter #79, Region 4
Charter Date: July 12, 1963

The Evansville Chapter was chartered in July of 1963. One charter member, Joyce Goebel, is still very active in the chapter and is the current chapter president. Evansville has hosted Forums and Annual Planning Conferences. Community service includes Habitat for Humanity, Block-Kids and CAD contests. In 2002, we won first place in Igloo's national contest.

Gr. Des Moines, Iowa
Chapter #80, Region 13
Charter Date: July 20, 1963

The Gr. Des Moines Chapter was chartered on July 20, 1963, with 29 members. The Quad Cities/Moline Chapter was the sponsor. National President Florence Creighton of St. Louis presented the charter. The chapter has produced a national region director, sponsored three other chapters and hosted a Forum. Currently, the chapter actively supports its local Rebuilding Together effort and New Directions, a women's shelter. We hold an annual golf outing to raise scholarship funds for Iowa State University's Construction Industry Program. We also hold a Block-Kids event to promote the industry to school-age kids in the Greater Des Moines area.

Durham, North Carolina
Chapter #83, Region 11
Charter Date: February 22, 1964

The Durham Chapter was chartered on February 22, 1964. We were the first chapter chartered in region 11 and have sponsored the chartering of Raleigh, N.C.; Greensboro, N.C.; Charlotte, N.C.; Fayetteville, N.C.; and Wilson, N.C. Service projects are related and beneficial to the construction industry and our communities. We participate in local association events to promote membership and create an awareness of NAWIC.

Dayton, Ohio
Chapter #85, Region 4
Charter Date: March 14, 1964

The Dayton Chapter is 41 years old. We have had many great experiences, formed lasting memories and served the Dayton area through education, scholarships and numerous networking opportunities. We have sponsored Career Days in conjunction with the Dayton City Schools, had Block-Kids programs and worked with Tri-State Construction Career Days. We have directed our efforts to promoting NAWIC to younger women working in the construction industry. We have also had a variety of interesting speakers covering topics from OSHA, to team building, and celebrating women. In increasing our membership we also look forward to increased involvement in community projects, especially those directed to women.

Columbus, Ohio
Chapter #86, Region 4
Charter Date: April 18, 1964

In September 1963, Dorothy Combs stumbled upon an article entitled, "Women Can Wear Hard Hats, Too." It was the story of a 10-year-old association called NAWIC. The article discussed the group's objectives and goals. The article inspired Dorothy to charter a chapter in Columbus, Ohio. On April 18, 1964, with the help of the Cincinnati, Ohio, Chapter, she did. In September 1964, at the NAWIC National Convention in Memphis, Tenn., the Columbus, Ohio, Chapter was given a "Certificate of Appreciation" for recruiting the most members that year — 64 in '64! The world has changed since 1964, but the need for this chapter and this organization is still strong.

Gr. Palm Beach, Florida
Chapter #87, Region 3
Charter Date: April 18, 1964

The Gr. Palm Beach Chapter was chartered on April 18, 1964. We have persevered through good and bad times. When our chapter began, our area was seasonal for construction. Since the '70s construction in general has become a major local economic force. Those changes in the industry have paralleled changes in our chapter. Our original members were mostly secretaries, clerks and office personnel. Today's membership reflects the acceptance of women in the work force — we now have general contractors, engineers, architects, accountants and more. We hope to continue to expand our diverse membership into the future.

Salt Lake City, Utah
Chapter #90, Region 8
Charter Date: May 9, 1964

1964 was a prominent year for the world and Utah. That year, the Beatles first appeared on Ed Sullivan; Martin Luther King, Jr., was awarded the Nobel Peace Prize; Soviet Union leader Nikita Khrushchev fell from power; and the 90th NAWIC chapter was chartered in Utah with 24 members. Margaret Borg was the chartering chapter secretary, and in 1969, she became NAWIC national president. The chapter was a pilot chapter for both Block-Kids and CAD and continues to sponsor these programs annually. This year, the chapter will sponsor its first Construction Fair for 7th graders in the state of Utah.

Orange County, California
Chapter #91, Region 12
Charter Date: June 6, 1964

The Orange County Chapter chartered on June 6, 1964, and is 40 years old. One founding member, Kathryn Clay, 92, is still active in the chapter. The charter banquet was at the Disney Hotel with 100 in attendance. Women wore white dresses and red rose corsages. A prime rib dinner was $4.00. Combined national and chapter dues were $10, and members wore uniforms. In the 1980s, membership numbers were as high as 84. The fashion show fund raiser was a trademark of the chapter for many years, and by popular demand is being resurrected in 2005.

Marin County, California
Chapter #94, Region 10
Charter Date: July 26, 1964

Raleigh, North Carolina
Chapter #92, Region 11
Charter Date: June 20, 1964

In 1963, Reek Fox with Dodge Reports attended a Peden Steel Company Open House. She was introduced to Frank Walters, with an Atlanta firm, who inquired if she knew about NAWIC. Reek was immediately interested in learning more. Subsequently, Reek received a letter detailing WIC and asked if she would lay the groundwork in organizing a Raleigh Chapter. In February 1964, Reek attended a Durham Chapter chartering banquet. Later, Durham sponsored the Raleigh Chapter chartering on June 20, 1964. The chapter chartered with 32 members. Reek Fox was the chartering president. Another instrumental member was Maggie Nelson, who is still a member today.

Wilmington, Delaware
Chapter #96, Region 1
Charter Date: January 14, 1964

Over the years, the chapter has sponsored blueprint reading courses, trade shows, Block-Kids and CAD courses. We give a scholarship annually and hold an industry appreciation meeting. We have participated in Habitat for Humanity Women Build. We have participated in community service projects with food drives and other events. Our chapter has offered support in hard times; friendships that have lasted for years; knowledge that is shared unselfishly; and confidence that each member can accomplish much more than she ever imagined.

Louisville, Kentucky
Chapter #97, Region 4
Charter Date: February 27, 1965

The Louisville Chapter hosted the 1984 National Convention. Jean Bokman was chapter president.

Greater Phoenix, Arizona
Chapter #98, Region 8
Charter Date: March 6, 1965

Perhaps the greatest accomplishment of the Greater Phoenix Chapter is its *Construction Dictionary©*. On Mother's Day, in 1966, more than 2,000 hours were contributed to the first edition of the dictionary. Five hundred copies of the spiral-bound paperback were made and were completely sold within three weeks. We are eternally grateful to the women who had the vision and the determination to make the *Construction Dictionary©* a reality and cherish and safeguard our legacy! The Greater Phoenix Chapter awards scholarships to female students at the three Arizona universities and is currently working on the 10th edition of the *Construction Dictionary©*.

Santa Clara, California
Chapter #99, Region 10
Charter Date: April 27, 1965

The Santa Clara Chapter is celebrating its 40th birthday this year. Our chapter was chartered in 1965, and June Simmons served as our chartering president. As a tribute to June, our scholarship fund retains her name. Our chapter is dedicated to promoting education to those pursuing a career in construction and/or related fields, and we strive to give out at least two scholarships a year. The Santa Clara Chapter believes in the core values of NAWIC and will be around for many years to come.

Greater Kansas City, Missouri
Chapter #100, Region 6
Charter Date: May 1, 1965

While the faces may have changed through the years, the chapter's goal remains the same: to enhance the success of women in the construction industry. We do this by providing programs, services and activities for women in the construction industry and by being the recognized source to champion women in the construction industry. Congratulations, from the Greater Kansas City Chapter for 50 years of proven commitment to women in the construction industry.

Greenville, South Carolina
Chapter #104, Region 11
Charter Date: June 5, 1965

The Greenville Chapter was chartered on June 5, 1965, with a growth in membership every year. We have participated in civic and construction projects over the years, including working with Habitat for Humanity. The annual golf tournament raises funds to support three scholarships awarded to tech students majoring in the field of construction. We've had two national winners in the CAD Drafting contest. We also hold Block-Kids contests with elementary school students.

Milwaukee, Wisconsin
Chapter #105, Region 13
Charter Date: June 19, 1965

In 1964, a few women interested in NAWIC contacted the Chicago, Ill., Chapter. An open house was held, and four women committed to the founding of a local chapter. These founding members represented the banking/bonding field and various positions in general contracting. The Milwaukee Chapter was charted in 1965. Our chapter started small and has grown to our current membership of 37. Our members are business owners and employees in the trades, administration, sales, architecture and engineering areas of construction. Our chapter sponsors community education programs for children and has adopted a group home for mentally challenged adults.

Fresno, California
Chapter #108, Region 10
Charter Date: July 17, 1965

Sponsored by the San Francisco, Calif., and Oakland, Calif., Chapters, the Fresno Chapter received its charter on July 17, 1965. From the original 21 members, its membership has soared to a high of 55 and settled at its present count of 31 members. The chapter has had four national officers: Marilyn Camin, CIT, NAWIC President 1984-1985 and NAWIC Director 2004-2006; Pauline McIntosh, CCA, CIT, NAWIC Director 2002-2004; Denise Redmond Crossland, CCA, NAWIC Director 1996-1998; and Carole Ponchetti, CCA, CIT, NAWIC Director 1982-1983. We are also proud to have had 10 members achieve their certifications for CCA, CIT or both.

Gr. Greensboro, North Carolina
Chapter #109, Region 11
Charter Date: July 17, 1965

The Gr. Greensboro Chapter was established in 1965. In the early days, as you can see in the picture of our lovely ladies, the chapter established its presence in Greensboro. As Greensboro grew, so did the reach of our chapter, now serving the Greater Greensboro area or the Piedmont of North Carolina. From the early days until now, construction plays a role in all things. We have been active with the Victory Junction Gang Camp, our most recent construction industry/civic project serving very sick children and their families.

San Gabriel Valley, California
Chapter #110, Region 12
Charter Date: August 14, 1965

Our chapter was chartered with the San Bernardino/ Riverside, Calif., Chapter on August 14, 1965. We have installed 30 presidents who have guided our chapter with vision and dedication. Some of these have passed on, but their memories are alive in the spirit of our chapter…like the memory about a NAWIC event held on a ship that was a lot of fun, and no one wanted to leave the ship. The band played a tune to which the master of ceremonies led everyone off the ship in a conga line. As we celebrate our 40th Anniversary, we look forward to making more memories and history with NAWIC.

San Bernardino-Riverside, California
Chapter #111, Region 12
Charter Date: August 14, 1965

Metropolitan Denver, Colorado
Chapter #112, Region 8
Charter Date: August 14, 1965

The Metropolitan Denver Chapter is a hard act to follow. The chapter has earned a reputation for hospitality on every level— twice hosting the NAWIC National Convention. Granted its charter on August 14, 1965, 10 years after the birth of NAWIC, the chapter has traditionally been non-traditional and innovative. The chapter chartered with 25 enthusiastic members. Today, Hazel J. Bolsover, CCA, CIT, a chartering member, is still active. Denver's Block-Kids contest winners have earned regional, national and NOVA-award successes. In addition to community and NEF contributions, Denver has its own scholarship program, which has awarded more than $100,000 to scholarship recipients pursuing construction-related education.

Columbia, South Carolina
Chapter #113, Region 11
Charter Date: August 21, 1965

The Columbia Chapter was chartered on August 21, 1965, with 23 members. Three of the charter members are still active, with a total membership of 74. The chapter maintains scholarship funds for students entering in the construction industry. Mary H. Clark established the first fund. We host an annual golf tournament to raise funds for our chapter. The chapter participates in numerous civic and construction projects from renovating hospitals to holding a two-week camp for teenagers. "Rosie's Girls" allow teens to take part in welding, carpentry, electrical work and other construction-related tasks.

Honolulu, Hawaii
Chapter #114, Region 12
Charter Date: November 27, 1965

The Honolulu Chapter had its beginnings in November of 1965. The idea that women of Hawaii's construction industry participate actively in its leadership has become a reality. Kathryn Clay, member of Region 10 Extension Committee, wrote to Hawaii's Congresswoman and explained the value of NAWIC. She was enthusiastic and initiated the Honolulu chapter of Women in Construction through the managers of the General Contractors Association of Hawaii. It was chartered on September 27, 1965, with 18 members.

Gr. Omaha, Nebraska
Chapter #116, Region 13
Charter Date: January 22, 1966

We were chartered in January of 1966 and are celebrating our 40th anniversary in 2005. We started out in Region 6 and are now a part of Region 13. The size of our chapter has fluctuated throughout the years, but our members have always kept our chapter strong, even when the numbers were small. Our main events every year are our golf outing to raise money for our scholarships and Block-Kids contests. The highlight of last year's contest was that the Region 13 winner and National 2nd place winner was our own Tommy Owens.

Danville, Illinois
Chapter #118, Region 6
Charter Date: February 19, 1966

The Danville Chapter was chartered on February 19, 1966, with 37 charter members, two of which are still active members. Those two members are Gail Kimball and Clara Kizer. Grace Dollens, who was the first vice president and also extension chairman of the Indianapolis, Ind., Chapter at that time, did the installation of our officers and presented the president's pin to our first president, Minnette Michaelson.

Gr. Wichita, Kansas
Chapter #120, Region 6
Charter Date: March 26, 1966

Chartered in 1966, the Gr. Wichita Chapter grew by leaps and bounds, with more and bigger events and activities every year. In the past, the chapter has conducted fund raisers, blueprint reading courses, Introduction to Construction courses, CPR classes and more. Over the years, the chapter has awarded more than $80,000 in scholarships. It is still a vibrant, energetic group, active in community events and striving to be a vital force in bringing recognition and support to all women in the construction industry.

Charlotte, North Carolina
Chapter #121, Region 11
Charter Date: April 16, 1966

The Charlotte Chapter was chartered on April 16, 1966, with 54 members as a chapter in Region 2. Region 11 was established the next year, so the chapter became a part of Region 11. The chapter has representation at the national and regional levels, resulting in strong leadership and a viable group involved in many worthwhile construction and community-related projects. A highlight of our year is a site visit to a significant project in our area.

Tucson, Arizona
Chapter #122, Region 8
Charter Date: April 23, 1966

The Tucson Chapter is making a difference. It recently gave an endowment of $11,000 to the Project for Homemakers in Arizona Seeking Employment (PHASE). This endowment is for women locally pursuing a construction-related career. The endowment is named after charter member Shirley Dail. PHASE serves about 600 displaced homemakers in Southern Arizona each year. Construction trades are popular among the clients of PHASE. The Tucson Chapter hopes to help women in the beginning of their new careers to purchase specialty tools or proper clothing needed to begin work in the construction trades.

Akron, Ohio
Chapter #124, Region 4
Charter Date: May 16, 1966

The Akron Chapter was chartered in May 1966. We had 60 members. We were chartered by the Cincinnati, Ohio, Chapter. Our chapter has chartered the Cleveland and Toledo, Ohio Chapters. We have two charter members who are still very active in the chapter: Evelyn Jones and Gloria Litwiller. Our chapter will hold its 27th Annual Style Show this April. The picture is from when the chapter hosted the Region 4 Forum.

Fox Valley, Wisconsin
Chapter #131, Region 13
Charter Date: August 13, 1966

The chapter chartered in August 1966 and was sponsored by the Milwaukee, Wis., Chapter, with 28 chartering members. We celebrated 35 years in 2001. Many scholarship awards have been given to students at U.W. Fox Valley through unique fund raisers, including pig roasts and an auction of the pig's head. At our meetings, we have a wide range of programs from site tours to Feng Shui. We are active in our community with donations at Christmas to the Salvation Army and local nursing homes. Our chapter has struggled and at one time had only four members. However, we continue to thrive with new ideas and members.

Columbus, Georgia
Chapter #134, Region 2
Charter Date: February 18, 1967

The Columbus Chapter was chartered on February 18, 1967, with 23 members, and Miss Jo Ann Crowder served as our first president. The chapter has been active in the community, the region and nationally. The chapter has sponsored construction courses, Block-Kids contests, drafting competitions and helped with Habitat for Humanity. The chapter has also awarded numerous scholarships to students studying in the construction field.

Baltimore, Maryland
Chapter #135, Region 1
Charter Date: March 18, 1967

Since its start in 1967, the Baltimore Chapter has continued to grow in both numbers and diversity. The incredible women that make up this chapter are brought together by a diverse knowledge of the construction industry. Having such a wide range of occupations and knowledge, these women bring a new and refreshing attitude to an industry once only known for its "strong men." Our chapter continues to grow each month, and we look forward to the continued success, not only of our chapter but also of the thousands of women who make up the organization and the industry. Congratulations, NAWIC, on your 50th anniversary!

Gr. Tidewater, Virginia
Chapter #137, Region 11
Charter Date: April 29, 1967

The Gr. Tidewater Chapter was chartered on April 29, 1967, with 62 members. Four charter members are still active - they are Louise Burnette, Margaret Eure, Nan Smith and Bobbie Harford.

Networking in NAWIC allows you to meet ladies from many construction firms like general contractors, suppliers, architects and engineers. These ladies are the best friends you can have.

We participate in many projects – Block-Kids, Habitat for Humanity, Samaritan House and more. We've held educational seminars, blueprint reading courses and estimating courses. Our annual golf tournaments are very successful and help fund our scholarship and other projects.

We are 38 years old this year and still going strong!

Ventura-Oxnard, California
Chapter #139, Region 12
Charter Date: May 20, 1967

The Los Angeles, Calif., Chapter chartered the Ventura-Oxnard Chapter on May 20, 1967. Our chapter chartered with 37 members. Today, we are honored to have Rosalee Asbell as an active member. Our membership has fluctuated from 20-50 members. Our chapter has included three regional directors and two national officers. Our one "claim to fame" was that we held the very first "Skirts 'n Dirt" in NAWIC. Our members actually got to operate and run various pieces of heavy, earth-moving equipment.

Pomona Valley, California
Chapter #140, Region 12
Charter Date: May 26, 1967

The Pomona Valley Chapter was chartered on May 26, 1967. The chapter has the dubious distinction of having one of its original charter members still active — Delores Whelchel. She worked in the HVAC industry for years before retiring, but she still is an integral part of our chapter. She has served in every position on the Board at least twice, and her home is affectionately called the "NAWIC Clubhouse," as most of the monthly board meetings are still held there.

Topeka, Kansas
Chapter #142, Region 6
Charter Date: June 3, 1967

The Topeka Chapter chartered on June 3, 1967, with eight members; we currently have 12. We may be small, but we are mighty. We participate in NEF Programs such as Block-Kids and CAD. We have helped build two Habitat "Women Build" houses. We have participated in community service projects, job site tours, job fairs and educational programs. This year will be our 30th Annual Golf Scholarship Tournament. Over the years, scholarship dollars have been awarded to Kansas State University, University of Kansas and Pittsburgh State University. Our goal is to spread the word of NAWIC to employers, which will grow our membership.

Richmond, Virginia
Chapter #141, Region 11
Charter Date: May 27, 1967

The Richmond Chapter came into being on May 27, 1967, with 40 charter members. This chapter was established largely due to the efforts of Margaret Watkins, now deceased, of the Richmond Builders' Exchange. Eva Poling was the installing national officer, and her chapter — the Greater Washington, D.C., Chapter — was our sponsoring chapter. The chapter was incorporated in 1969 as a nonprofit corporation. We have hosted three Fall Planning Conferences. We have hosted four Spring Forums. The Richmond Chapter has chartered three chapters in Virginia.

Spokane, Washington
Chapter #143, Region 9
Charter Date: June 10, 1967

The Spokane Chapter was chartered in June 1967. Charter members Donna Meidling, Carolyn Pierce and Peggy Grewe still belong to the chapter. The chapter has had two national officers: Donna Meidling served as National Treasurer and National President; Chris Wigginton served as National Secretary. Five Region 9 Directors hailed from Spokane: Donna Meidling, Torchy Gordon, Leslie Rendle, Chris Wigginton and Midge Logan. The chapter chartered or co-chartered the following chapters: Billings and Great Falls, Mont.; Anchorage and Fairbanks, Alaska; Boise and Lewiston, Idaho; and Tri-Cities and Yakima, Wash. The chapter has hosted six Regional Forums and several Regional Planning Conferences in its 37-year history.

Philadelphia, Pennsylvania
Chapter #145, Region 1
Charter Date: July 15, 1967

Chartered in 1967, the chapter has remained strong. Two of the original charter members, Eileen Franzosa and Patricia Gibbons, are active members and have been serving on our Board for a number of years. Over the years, the Philadelphia Chapter has chartered six chapters; had a National Secretary, Eleanor Buckley; had two Regional Directors, Eleanor Buckley and Lucille Radomski; hosted Annual Planning Conferences and Forums; and even hosted the National Convention in 1976. We are proud to say we have given out scholarships every year for more than 35 years and have participated in the Block-Kids competition every year since its inception.

San Fernando Valley, California
Chapter #153, Region 12
Charter Date: May 11, 1968

This California chapter has been cheering on the construction industry for more than 30 years. We represent the valley near Los Angeles, which was once endless orange groves and now is the home to movie studios, the Budweiser Factory, several universities and millions of people. Our chapter meets the fourth Tuesday of the month. We have a history of sponsoring educational programs, giving scholarships and working with the community. We've put on events of all kinds from golf tournaments, to a spaghetti tree fund raiser, to casino nights and tours of construction sites.

Asheville, North Carolina
Chapter #154, Region 11
Charter Date: June 28, 1968

The Asheville, N.C., Chapter was chartered on June 28, 1968, with 23 members. The chapter has remained small but has been active in many projects. Our chapter renovated a duplex that was used as Asheville's first shelter for battered women. We worked to help finish our local homeless shelter. Presently, we wrap gifts at Christmas to benefit Hospice. The Asheville Chapter is probably unique in the fact that member Lois Davis has served 18 terms as president. She has passed the gavel on several times to her daughter, Lisa Slechter, who is presently serving her 8th term as president. The chapter has won many awards, including one award for "Chapter With The Biggest Heart."

Cleveland, Ohio
Chapter #156, Region 4
Charter Date: July 13, 1967

In speaking with present and former members, their favorite memories include attending Forums, hosting Forums, community projects and general meetings. Most of all, our past and present members' greatest benefit and favorite times seemed to be the "sisterhood" formed between members — the true feeling of belonging to a group that accepts you for who you are and does not judge because you are a woman in construction. Women wear that title with pride. We are a chapter that concentrates on education, community service and most of all — sisterhood! We are proud to be members of NAWIC, and we say it, "Loud and Proud!"

Cedar Rapids–Iowa City, Iowa
Chapter #160, Region 13
Charter Date: February 22, 1969

This chapter was chartered in February 1969, with 24 members. The chapter is involved at the regional and national level. We hold an annual NAWIC golf tournament every year. We have standing reservations from year to year, and it is our biggest fund raiser. Our chapter is involved in community service projects such as a scholarship fund and an annual Block-Kids competition, which receive tremendous support from the local construction industry. Kathy Enabnit was five years old when she attended her first meeting. Years later, she became chapter president.

St. Joseph, Missouri
Chapter #162, Region 6
Charter Date: May 3, 1969

Charter date: May 3, 1969, at the Hotel Robidoux in downtown St. Joseph.
First President: Jean Mecke.
Chapter History: 1971 — Second place NAWIC scrapbook; 1972 — First scholarship awarded, recipient was Richard LaFollett; 1974 — Delegation to Jefferson City, Missouri, where Governor Kit Bond signed WIC Week Proclamation; 1975 — Award for largest percent increase in membership in region; 1995 — Leader in Chapter Membership Growth Award; 1995 — First Block-Kids Competition; 1998 — Hosted Region 6 Forum; 2001 — Second place Professional Education Award; 2004-2005 Officers: President — Amy Stanton, CIT; Vice President — Sara Markt, CIT; Secretary — Sally Higbe, CIT; Treasurer — Heidi Walker, CIT.

Pittsburgh, Pennsylvania
Chapter #161, Region 1
Charter Date: March 29, 1969

This photo was taken May 16, 1981, when the mayor of Pittsburgh, Richard S. Caliguiri (now deceased), proclaimed "Women in Construction Day" in the City of Pittsburgh "in recognition of the contributions made by the women in the construction industry to the civic, educational and economic well-being of our community; to focus attention on the special activities planned this day by the Pittsburgh Chapter No. 161." The NAWIC members in the photograph, left to right, are Bernice Jenkins, Barbara Koronowski, Sue Ingold, Joyce Wintgens and Evelyn Miller.

Minneapolis/St. Paul, Minnesota
Chapter #164, Region 13
Charter Date: June 7, 1969

Hartford, Connecticut
Chapter #165, Region 1
Charter Date: June 7, 1969

Thirty-six years of leading by example with selfless dedication and commitment to further the objectives — to unite, promote, encourage and provide — with the willingness to participate, share and explore new possibilities — to bring about a better understanding of the industry and support the women within it. The members of the Hartford Chapter can be proud of its accomplishments over the years and for its active involvement, at all levels, within the Association, and at promoting the construction industry — 36 years of growing, changing and sustaining the times.

Monterey County, California
Chapter #167, Region 10
Charter Date: June 21, 1969

The Monterey County Chapter celebrated its 35th Anniversary last year. The Chapter (formerly called Monterey Peninsula) had its first meeting at the Monterey Builders Exchange in June of 1969. The first installation of officers took place at the Del Monte Hyatt in Monterey with 20 members. Today, our chapter still has 20 members, including three charter members. Our members make a difference by contributing to other construction organizations in the county and state. The chapter functions have benefited many organizations from a local homeless shelter and school career fair to the Monterey Bay Girl and Boy Scouts. We look forward to many more years of service.

Fayetteville, North Carolina
Chapter #168, Region 11
Charter Date: June 28, 1969

The chapter chartered on June 28, 1969. The Fayetteville Chapter has held Annual Forums, Annual Planning Conferences and has been very involved in the community through volunteering and participating in Block-Kids and CAD/Design/Drafting competitions. Frances Jackson, CIT, (pictured) is the current chapter president and was a charter member of the chapter. She has served as Region 11 Director, on national NAWIC committees and has been very involved with NEF, most recently serving as its president in 2003-2004. The Fayetteville chapter is proud of its accomplishments to its community and to women working in construction. The chapter looks forward to celebrating its 40th anniversary in 2009.

Buffalo, New York
Chapter #172, Region 14
Charter Date: February 7, 1970

Our chapter was chartered in February of 1970. The chapter was a part of Region 1 until Region 14 was formed. We were the first chapter chartered in New York. We currently have 22 members. Each year, the chapter awards a $1,000 scholarship to a student in a construction-related field and exposes many students to construction through Block-Kids. Chapter events have included a Risk Management Boot Camp and a 10-Hour OSHA Safety Course. We hold an annual auction with a portion of the proceeds donated to a charitable cause or used toward our community projects.

San Luis Obispo, California
Chapter #174, Region 12
Charter Date: June 27, 1970

The chapter was chartered on June 27, 1970, with 50 members. Through the years, we have been involved with various community-service and outreach projects. We have participated in professional education endeavors and helped enhance the success of women in their chapter. The chapter has awarded many scholarships to students pursuing construction-related degrees. Today, the chapter continues to be a voice for women in construction in California.

Lansing, Michigan
Chapter #177, Region 4
Charter Date: February 20, 1971

The Lansing Chapter was chartered on February 20, 1971, with 29 members. The first chapter to charter in 1971, the first chapter to charter in the state and the first to be chartered by Region 4. We participated in our first Women Build project in June of 2000. Our members donated their time and efforts to help in constructing this new home.

Bakersfield, California
Chapter #182, Region 12
Charter Date: July 24, 1971

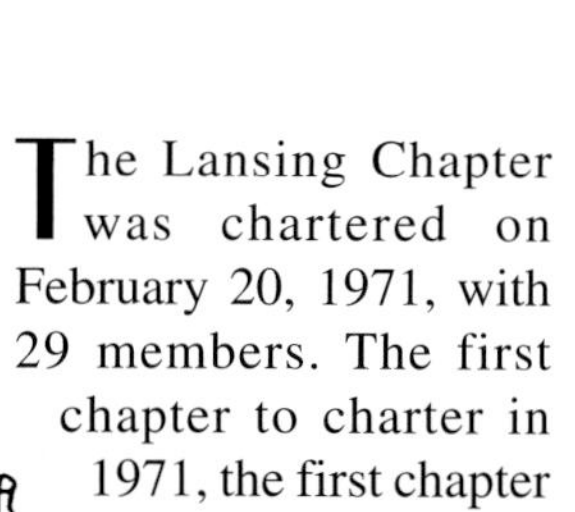

The Bakersfield Chapter was chartered on July 24, 1971. We are very proud that Lillian Valenti, our chartering President, continues her membership in our chapter. Our Board of Directors meets the first Wednesday of each month, and general membership meetings are held on the third Thursday. Our yearly goals are established by the membership on the recommendations of the Strategic Planning Committee and as ratified by the Board of Directors. Close attention is given to compliance with national guidelines, and we keep in mind the vision of what we as women can do to promote education in the industry.

Detroit, Michigan
Chapter #183, Region 4
Charter Date: October 16, 1971

The Detroit Chapter of NAWIC celebrated our 33rd year in 2004. Our members include tradeswomen, architects, engineers and attorneys to name a few. The chapter has participated in a number of events through the years, including "Paint the Town!" home remodeling projects, Habitat projects, playground construction, Block-Kids contests, annual Construction Industry Night and more!

Tacoma, Washington
Chapter #187, Region 9
Charter Date: March 11, 1972

With 28 charter members, the Seattle, Wash., Chapter helped charter the chapter on March 11, 1972. The chapter still has one active charter member, Marie Gustin. The chapter has produced many Region 9 Directors, Regional WICs of the Year and other award winners. We even have a national president from our chapter – Sandra Glassie, 1986-1987. We are active in Block-Kids and give local scholarships each year. Members are active in Habitat's Women Builds and support the "Family Renewal Shelter" for battered women and children. We are dedicated to enhancing the success of women in the construction industry.

O'Hare Suburban, Illinois
Chapter #193, Region 13
Charter Date: October 18, 1972

Chartered October 28, 1972, the O'Hare Suburban Chapter has enhanced the careers of many women in the northwest suburbs of Chicago. The chapter is proud to acknowledge Past Region Directors Thelma Faulstitch and Harriet Reilly. Member Helen Adams was elected national treasurer in the mid-1980s. In 1999, Denise Norberg-Johnson was elected national president. In 1991, the chapter created the O'Hare Scholarship Endowment Fund (OSEF): a separate entity to provide scholarships to students in construction-related fields. O'Hare has distributed more than $80,000 over the last 32 years. Today, we have 26 chapter members with four regional committee chairs.

Tri-Cities, Washington
Chapter #192, Region 9
Charter Date: August 19, 1972

On August 19, 1972, the Tri-Cities Chapter was charted with 30 members by the Spokane, Wash., Chapter. Region 9 Director-Elect Donna Meidling installed the chapter officers: President — Thelma Charles; Vice President — Freda Stromstad; Secretary — Judy McKenzie; and Treasurer — Verda Carney. National President-Elect Janith Gould was also in attendance. Currently, the membership is growing again from a low of 8 members to 14 current members. I am proud to say we currently have 90 percent participation at events.

Grand Rapids, Michigan
Chapter #194, Region 4
Charter Date: February 17, 1973

The chapter was founded on February 17, 1973. Since then, the Grand Rapids chapter has made its mark in West Michigan through various endeavors, including chartering the Kalamazoo/Battle Creek Chapter; awarding more than $90,000; actively partnering with Minority Contractors Association of West Michigan, Construction Association of Michigan, Construction Specifications Institute – Grand Rapids, and American Society of Professional Estimators; participating in construction industry trade shows; and supporting and mentoring Construction Management students at Ferris State University. We currently have two charter members and member representation for every division within the construction industry. Membership averages about 30 members.

Anchorage, Alaska
Chapter #197, Region 9
Charter Date: June 13, 1973

The Anchorage Chapter was chartered on June 13, 1973, and was incorporated in the state of Alaska on May 24, 1982, with one chartering member remaining a member until 2003. Three chapter members have become Region 9 Director and one succeeded in becoming the 42nd NAWIC president. The chapter has been active in the community participating in programs such as Block-Kids, CAD/Drafting, Christmas in May, Construction Garage Sale, Alaska AGC Annual Conference, and has teamed with SWE, ASID and the Alaska Tradeswomen on several events. The chapter has received numerous national awards including Construction Industry, Chapter Excellence and Professional Education.

Salem, Oregon
Chapter #198, Region 9
Charter Date: June 23, 1973

In 1973, the Salem Chapter chartered with the Portland, Oreg., Chapter sponsoring. The chapter chartered with 43 members. In the early stages of our chapter, we were helped monetarily by AGC. AGC also provided speakers. Since then, our focus has been on educating our members, informing students of the opportunities in construction and community participation. We currently have 25 members. This year will be our second annual Construction Career Days in partnership with Salem Keizer schools, ODOT and the Federal Highway Administration. This is a hands-on event where 500 high school kids can try their hands at running large equipment, brick and concrete work, carpentry, electrical and plumbing.

Paducah, Kentucky
Chapter #201, Region 4
Charter Date: March 23, 1974

The Paducah Chapter chartered on March of 1974. The chapter currently has six members. We have been involved in many community activities such as Spouse Abuse, Christmas in April and Habitat for Humanity. We have built floats for the Labor Day and Christmas Parades. We work together with AGC and Homebuilders on various activities. We provide scholarships to local students in a construction-related program. We provide groceries for a needy family at Thanksgiving and Christmas. In addition, at Christmas we furnish Santa for a needy family.

Southwest Cook County, Illinois
Chapter #205, Region 13
Charter Date: June 29, 1974

Central Pennsylvania
Chapter #208, Region 1
Charter Date: September 7, 1974

In 1974, our charter members had the vision to believe in themselves and form the Central Pennsylvania Chapter, formerly called the "York-Lancaster Chapter." The chapter set the standard curriculum for the Construction Drafting Design programs with Brownstown Vo-Tech. Since the mid '80s, the chapter has awarded more than $13,000 in scholarships to aspiring construction industry youth. The chapter's 30th Anniversary Celebration was held November 16, 2004. More than 100 years of cumulative chapter service were represented at the celebration.

Coachella Valley, California
Chapter #212, Region 12
Charter Date: March 15, 1975

The Coachella Valley Chapter was chartered on March 15, 1975. Eloise Dunphy served as our chartering president. She is still active in the chapter even though she is more than 80 years old. We are celebrating our 30th year in 2005. Through the years, the remaining members have been loyal to NAWIC, NEF and Region 12. We have been educated far more than we thought possible — this is a journey we are so glad we didn't miss.

Long Beach Area, California
Chapter #210, Region 12
Charter Date: November 16, 1974

The Long Beach Area Chapter was chartered in November of 1974. Happily, we still have active charter members. The chapter's original name was "Mid-Cities/Los Angeles County." Later we became "Mid-Cities." As the city of Los Angeles grew, the need to become the "Long Beach Area" Chapter became apparent. We participate in the CAD and Block-Kids contests. And, with the help of our sponsors and supporters, we have been able to award many scholarships over the years. Each chapter member is very grateful to those women in Fort Worth for giving birth to this wonderful organization.

Greater Everett, Washington
Chapter #213, Region 9
Charter Date: May 31, 1975

The Greater Everett Chapter is located in Everett, Wash., and was granted a charter on May 31, 1975. Of the 27 founding members, two are included in the current roster, Diane (Hillis) Ferguson and Sandra Skolrud. Through the years, the organization has provided professional programs at the general meetings, including tours of the Everett Historical Theater, the Snohomish County Jail and speakers from many areas of the Construction Industry. Continuing education has been encouraged through scholarships and seminars, including Lien Laws, Blueprint Reading, CAD/Drafting Classes and Block-Kids. The chapter has provided workers for community projects such as Clothes for Kids and other workdays.

The Granite State, New Hampshire
Chapter #218, Region 14
Charter Date: August 23, 1975

Fond memories from Granite State Chapter members …

"I remember a feeling of gratification and success during 'Camp Compass' — a Career Day for middle-school girls."

"Many moons ago, I remember my first NAWIC conference that was in Great Gorge, N.J. We traveled with the Boston Chapter by bus. I have made many friends and have enjoyed many tours of different projects."

"I have made many friends, visited many places and learned so many new things. Thank you, NAWIC, for enhancing my life in so many ways."

Great Falls, Montana
Chapter #228, Region 9
Charter Date: May 22, 1976

Roanoke Valley, Virginia
Chapter #226, Region 11
Charter Date: May 15, 1976

This chapter chartered May 15, 1976, with 28 members. Through the years, we have hosted APCs, Forums and annual Block-Kids contests. Even during tough years, we never lost sight of our goals, and we are now an even stronger, larger and more productive chapter. We worked together as a team to grow our chapter. We hosted our first annual golf tournament in April of 2004, and we currently have 22 members. We look back on the past years with pride, and we look forward to the years to come with excitement and anticipation.

Greater Sioux Falls, South Dakota
Chapter #237, Region 13
Charter Date: June 4, 1977

The Sioux Falls Chapter was chartered on June 4, 1977, with 26 members. We are pleased that two of those members, Gert Dekker and Carole Lee, still remain members today. The first Block-Kids contest was held in 1993. The chapter participates in Women in Construction Week every year and a Career Fair. Other service projects include Habitat for Humanity and the Sioux Falls Paint-a-Thon. We also award scholarships yearly. We are pleased to have two past regional directors as current members. The Sioux Falls Chapter remains strong in its efforts to enhance the success of women in the construction industry.

Greater New York
Chapter #240, Region 1
Charter Date: August 6, 1977

The Greater New York Chapter was chartered on August 6, 1977, with 48 members. Chartering officers were Rose Gruppuso, Anne Avenius, Eileen Field and Joan Mehos. Two months later, the chapter hosted the APC for Region 1. In 1985, the Chapter hosted the NAWIC Annual Convention in New York City. Today, the chapter has more than 20 members and continues to meet monthly, most recently holding events with Habitat for Humanity and the IRS. Charter members Carol Ericson and Joan Mehos both served as NAWIC national president. Charter members Daisy Menkes-Klein and Joan Mehos maintain their membership today.

Boise, Idaho
Chapter #245, Region 9
Charter Date: March 18, 1978

The Boise Chapter was chartered March 18, 1978. It took 15 members to charter a chapter — the Boise Chapter chartered with almost 40 members. Membership declined in the '80s, but now, our numbers are strong, with between 50 and 60 members. We are fortunate to have one charter member still active, Mary Kaye Isle. Every year, the Boise Chapter holds several fund raisers, including a golf tournament and dinner auction. Our dinner auction just celebrated its 14th year and has grown from an attendance of 30 to more than 160, with the proceeds funding our chapter's scholarship program and many other community projects.

Greater Worcester, Massachusetts
Chapter #241, Region 14
Charter Date: August 20, 1977

Fargo-Moorhead, North Dakota
Chapter #246, Region 13
Charter Date: June 3, 1978

Members of the 2004–2005 Fargo-Moorhead "Construction Crew" are Andrea Abrahamson, Lynn D. Madaus, Norma Andersen, Ilene F. Osten, Amy Berg, Nancy Slotten, Carrie M. Bertsch, Sarah Sutter, Kyle Handegard, Dawn M. Wiedewitsch, Onie R. Loeks and Marcy J. Zimmerman.

El Paso, Texas
Chapter #248, Region 8
Charter Date: June 24, 1978

The El Paso Chapter was chartered in June of 1978. Members have donated their time, talents and building materials to make improvements at the Rape Crisis Center, the Child Crisis Center, the Insights Museum for Children, the Area 19 Special Olympics and the CASAs to name a few. In 2001, El Paso was the primary sponsor working with the Federal Highway Administration to bring Construction Career Days to west Texas, with more than 2,000 high school students attending from the surrounding areas. Our primary objectives are education and community service.

Lake Charles, Louisiana
Chapter #250, Region 5
Charter Date: July 22, 1978

The Lake Charles Chapter was chartered on July 22, 1978, with 28 members. Our chapter has been recognized for growth and retention; had the first Red Rose Recruiter in 1991, Donna Haynes, CIT; and is the home to current Region 5 Director Janice Law. Doris Young, chartering member and past chapter president, was honored at our 25th Anniversary Celebration. Our members give generously to NEF, conduct Block-Kids contests, participate in charitable events, raise scholarship funds and have fun! Our small chapter has stayed close because of the enduring friendships, mentoring and support system we have. Lake Charles is alive and well!

Delta Valley, California
Chapter #253, Region 10
Charter Date: August 26, 1978

The Delta Valley Chapter was founded in August 1978, and charter member Doris Specht is still going strong. We enjoy working together on our two annual fund raisers, a women's only golf tournament in September and a crab feed in January. Hands-on projects include renovations for Haven of Peace, a local women's shelter.

Simi-Conejo, California
Chapter #254, Region 12
Charter Date: October 14, 1978

In 2003, the chapter celebrated its 25th Anniversary and installation of officers. Nancy Eaton performed our candle ceremony, and our original chapter founders attended, along with the Ventura-Oxnard, Calif., Chapter. It was a very special evening. The chapter almost ended years ago, but the Ventura-Oxnard Chapter got involved and helped our chapter thrive again. We are happily up to 32 members and going forward with grand plans for the future!

Mississippi Gulf Coast
Chapter #256, Region 5
Charter Date: December 2, 1978

Erma Lamousin helped form the Mississippi Gulf Coast Chapter in 1978. Ms. Lamousin served on the Nativity Elementary School Board, and she had an idea to introduce elementary school-aged kids to construction. So, a group of members from Mississippi Gulf Coast Chapter presented "Block-Kids" to the school. The chapter organized the Block-Kids program, and the school had it as a fund raiser. The chapter held the Block-Kids program for two or three years with the school. Ms. Lamousin introduced the program to the NAWIC Board. Ms. Lamousin and the NAWIC Board worked together to create the Block-Kids guidelines.

Capital District, New York
Chapter #261, Region 14
Charter Date: February 17, 1979

This chapter started in 1979 with 21 charter members. The chapter organized with the purpose of providing women with a place to discuss issues unique to women in the construction field at a time when women were the exception rather than the rule. The chapter has awarded more than $12,000 in scholarships. We also have donated to The Ronald McDonald House, Albany Medical Center's Children's Hospital and the battered women's shelters in the capital region. Members have spoken to various groups to encourage women and men to enter the construction field. We have been sitting on the committee of Construction Career Days since its inception in 2002. Speakers from the area have kept us informed about changes within the industry.

Atlantic City, New Jersey
Chapter #258, Region 1
Charter Date: December 21, 1978

From our installation in 1978 at the first casino in Atlantic City to the present, it has certainly been an interesting ride. We have many fund raisers from fancy fashion shows to energetic golf tournaments. Our chapter has worked hard to give scholarships to local men and women, and we are quite proud of this achievement. We believe the event that was the most fulfilling and worthwhile was our October 26, 1991, Annual Planning Conference. The picture shows us pausing to smile in our Hospitality Room.

Vermont
Chapter #262, Region 14
Charter Date: March 10, 1979

The chapter chartered on March 10, 1979, with more than 50 members. The Granite State, N.H., Chapter was our sponsoring chapter. Just as we had help from The Granite State Chapter, we did the same for other organizations such as Northern New England Tradeswomen and the Child Care Apprenticeship Trust Fund. In more recent years, our membership numbers have dwindled, but the small group we have is still enthusiastic and active. Member Viola Leskinen served as Region 14 director, 1996-98 and went to China in 1998 with the NAWIC delegation. We participate in Block-Kids and award a college scholarship each year.

Montgomery, Alabama
Chapter #267, Region 2
Charter Date: June 9, 1979

The Montgomery Chapter was chartered on June 9, 1979. Our chapter has produced four region directors, a national secretary and numerous regional and national committee chairs. We conduct construction-related seminars and Block-Kids contests. During WIC Week, we receive proclamations from the governor of Alabama and from the mayor of Montgomery. We also sponsor "Ms. Fix-It Day" at The Home Depot. Also, we will be sponsoring a construction industry-wide blood drive this year. In keeping with NAWIC's core purpose, the Montgomery chapter awards several scholarships annually to deserving college students. We personally interview top applicants and present checks at our Executive Appreciation Night.

Black Hills, South Dakota
Chapter #269, Region 13
Charter Date: July 14, 1979

The Black Hills Chapter was chartered on July 14, 1979, in Rapid City, S.D., with 21 members. Nancy Ericksen was charter president and was instrumental in organizing the chapter. We have been involved in community service projects: Habitat for Humanity, Christmas in April, Women Against Violence, Highway Cleanup and an annual parade. Construction Industry projects include annual Block-Kids contest, AGC Construction Awareness and Career Days. The Black Hills Chapter hosted Region 13's Annual Forum in 1983, 1993 and 2003. We have been represented at all Annual Conventions, except one, in our 25-year history. We are proud to have five charter members still active.

Maine
Chapter #276, Region 14
Charter Date: August 25, 1979

We just celebrated our 25th Anniversary! Construction Expo of Maine is our most rewarding project, providing more than $200,000 in scholarships to Maine students pursuing a career in construction. The 2005 Expo will be our 25th. For many years, we entered the "Great Kennebec River Whatever Race." Members constructed a float, adapting it to each year's theme. Many awards were won and members completed the welding and artwork. Other projects have included playground construction, Career Days, liaisons with construction trade associations and promoting and participating in NEF programs. In 2001, we co-sponsored the National Tradeswomen Conference, sending nine members from Maine. Please visit our web site www.nawicmaine.org.

Rockford, Illinois
Chapter #277, Region 13
Charter Date: August 25, 1979

The Rockford Chapter became 25 years young this year. It doesn't seem possible. In the beginning, employers viewed NAWIC as a "Women's Club," but over the years, we have proved our worth to the industry. Our work with Block-Kids and CAD competitions has helped the industry appreciate and support our involvement. Our membership has fluctuated over the years, but we have remained a very enthusiastic group. Our chapter has been "very vocal" from the beginning regarding issues that were important to us, and we continue with that tradition today. We are a forward-looking chapter, and we are looking forward to a great future for NAWIC!

Yakima Valley, Washington
Chapter #279, Region 9
Charter Date: October 20, 1979

Northwest Arkansas
Chapter #280, Region 5
Charter Date: December 1, 1979

A fond memory … In 1984, the chapter held a Bosses' Night. The theme was the "Good 'Ole Days." Huge records from construction paper and glitter hung from the ceilings, and music played and dancing was everywhere. The ladies handmade programs that looked like records.

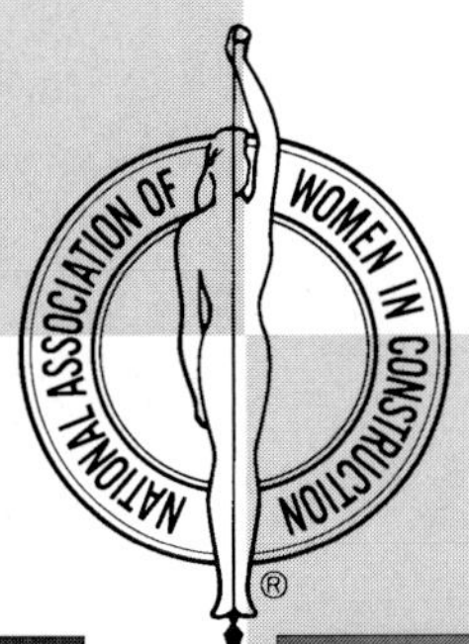

Toledo, Ohio
Chapter #282, Region 4
Charter Date: March 8, 1980

The Toledo Chapter was chartered in 1980 with 22 members. Currently, we have about 30 members that are very active in the community. Annually, we award college scholarships to deserving construction-related students in our area with more than $125,000 given to-date. We have participated in the CAD high school competition since 1995, and one of our students went on to win National. We have also conducted Block-Kids competitions for numerous years, with several of our members winning regional awards. Toledo has also worked on a Habitat "Women Build" home in 2003-2004 and participated in WIC Week.

Volusia County, Florida
Chapter #284, Region 3
Charter Date: February 2, 1980

We chartered in 1980 and are happy that two charter members, Bobbie Cheh and Mary Russell, are still active in our chapter. We're proud that we've achieved our 25th year by following NAWIC's lead. We've participated in NEF's educational programs and listened to excellent meeting speakers. We feel education has been the cornerstone of our chapter. Most recently, we hosted Region 3's Race to Daytona Forum. Best of all, NAWIC members become friends for life.

Norwich-New London, Connecticut
Chapter #291, Region 1
Charter Date: July 11, 1981

Since chartering in 1981, the chapter has always been a small – but mighty – chapter. We have put on a trades training program (PACTT) placing women in the construction industry after completion. We had a National winner in the Block-Kids program. We participated in several all women builds for Habitat for Humanity, and have hosted Regional APC's and Forums. We have received the Construction Advocacy Award, many Chapter Excellence awards and the Regional Superstar Award. We have done this with an average of nine enthusiastic members, and we wish all NAWIC members an enthusiastic — Happy 50th Anniversary!

Toronto, Ontario, Canada
Chapter #295, Region 14
Charter Date: June 5, 1982

The Toronto Chapter was chartered in 1982. In 1987, the Toronto Chapter, in partnership with the Ontario Women's directorate, produced "Women into Construction: A Blueprint for Action." The chapter hosted NAWIC's First International Convention in 1988, with approximately 1,200 members throughout North America in attendance. The Toronto Chapter hosted Regional Forums in 1995 and 2004. In 2000, in conjunction with other construction associations in Ontario, the chapter participated in the publishing of "The Future is Yours To Build: Ontario Construction Career Booklet." Community outreach includes an annual fund raiser for women's shelters and food banks.

Southwest Florida
Chapter #297, Region 3
Charter Date: July 30, 1982

Fifty years ago, 16 women had a vision in Fort Worth, Texas. That vision was carried to Southwest Florida in 1983 when 80 women chartered Chapter 297. For the last 22 years, members of our chapter have strived to educate, mentor and develop the success of women in construction. As we look back, one community project has come full circle. Our founding members played a vital role in the construction of the first shelter for Abuse and Counseling and Treatment Centers. Once again, we find ourselves with hard hats and gloves on, ready to meet their construction needs.

Long Island, New York
Chapter #300, Region 1
Charter Date: July 9, 1983

Myrtle Beach, South Carolina
Chapter #301, Region 11
Charter Date: August 6, 1983

The Myrtle Beach Chapter, sponsored by the Columbia, S.C., Chapter, was chartered as the Grand Stand, S.C., Chapter on August 6, 1983. The chapter name was changed to the Myrtle Beach, S.C., Chapter for better recognition of our area. Through trials, hard work and the perseverance of founding members, we have evolved into a very active and accomplished chapter. We are active in our community, work with other industry associations and have a billboard display during WIC Week. We have hosted two APCs and one Annual Forum. We have two Red Rose Recruiters, five CITs, one CDS and one region director from our chapter.

Kalamazoo/Battle Creek, Michigan
Chapter #302, Region 4
Charter Date: August 27, 1983

The Kalamazoo/Battle Creek Chapter will celebrate its 22nd anniversary in August 2005. Over the years, we have always believed in sharing the spirit and values of NAWIC through the support and mentoring of each other and by offering support to others in the industry. We are proud to have just completed our 14th consecutive Block-Kids contest and annually award a scholarship to any individual working in construction who applies for assistance. We have eight members who have completed their CCA, CDS or CIT certifications – quite an accomplishment for a chapter with only 11 members!

Terre Haute, Indiana
Chapter #303, Region 4
Charter Date: January 14, 1984

This photo was taken in January 2003 at our Anniversary dinner. Attendees included four ladies (seated) that were involved in the chartering event on January 14, 1984. The woman sitting to the far right became president at the time of chartering. At our dinner, she brought a photo album and numerous letters from NAWIC chapters, local companies, the city mayor and state governor congratulating us on that wonderful event. At our 20-year anniversary celebration in January 2004, we welcomed these ladies again, where the photo album was given to us as our new NAWIC keepsake celebrating our chapter history.

Wilmington, North Carolina
Chapter #308, Region 11
Charter Date: March 30, 1985

Northwest Indiana
Chapter #311, Region 4
Charter Date: May 18, 1985

Greater Rochester, New York
Chapter #314, Region 14
Charter Date: September 28, 1985

The Greater Rochester Chapter was chartered in 1985 and was sponsored by the Buffalo, N.Y., Chapter. We still have a joint meeting with the Buffalo Chapter at least once a year. We have adopted a mile of the Genesee Valley Greenway as one of our community projects. Every year, we host a Christmas Party for needy families at the Bethany House in Rochester, supplying food and gifts. We have built playgrounds, put on seminars and hosted both spring Forum and APC. We are home to past Region 14 Director Cari Durbin.

Tri County, Florida
Chapter #317, Region 3
Charter Date: January 18, 1986

Lorain County, Ohio
Chapter #320, Region 4
Charter Date: May 30, 1987

The Tri-County Chapter chartered on January 18, 1986, with approximately 35 members. We still have one charter member, Ann Wood. Sue Reed joined only six months later. Our scholarship fund, the Sue Davenport Memorial Scholarship Fund, is named after a charter member. We have given many scholarships over the years. Our Block-Kids competitions usually have about 125 children. We have participated in Habitat for Humanity, Adopt-a-Highway, Paint the Town, Safe Space (for battered women), Adopt-a-Family and food drives. We have had yard sales, bake sales, fashion shows, raffles and golf tournaments to support our chapter.

The Lorain County Chapter was chartered in 1987. To this day, we have seven charter members who are still active in the chapter. We have held Block-Kids competitions for the past 12 years and given scholarships to Lorain County Community College students for the last 13 years. Some of our construction projects include building park equipment, painting Boy Scout cabins and installing siding and shingles for Habitat's Women Build. And, of course, our greatest accomplishment – building a 2,000 square-foot home in the year 2000 in less than 2,000 minutes. For this event, all proceeds were given to the Genesis House for Battered Women and Children.

Coos/Douglas, Oregon
Chapter #324, Region 9
Charter Date: January 30, 1988

Antelope Valley, California
Chapter #327, Region 12
Charter Date: January 7, 1989

Chicago Metro, Illinois
Chapter #325, Region 13
Charter Date: March 26, 1988

The Chicago Metro Chapter celebrated its 15-year anniversary in 2003. We started with 38 members and are still going strong with 32, including two founding members. We focus on professional education for our members as well as working to help the community and construction industry. We hold an annual blueprint reading class. We are involved with Southwest Women Working Together, an organization helping abused women get in the work force through training that includes construction trades. We have also participated in Rebuilding Chicago. Our chapter congratulates NAWIC on its 50th Anniversary and hopes to help it reach 100 years.

Eastern Maine
Chapter #329, Region 14
Charter Date: November 18, 1989

The Eastern Maine Chapter was chartered on November 19, 1989, in Bangor, Maine. The chapter currently has seven members, of which three are charter members. Though the chapter is small, it is very powerful. In the past 15 years, the chapter has hosted two Spring Forums and an APC, held Introduction to Construction courses, a Construction Days event, Block-Kids, CAD, awarded scholarships and more. The chapter is always represented at all regional and national events. The members are *Sandy Ferguson, *Brenda King, Maren Mcgillicuddy, Jessica Oakman, Jackie Robinson, *Bev Rollins, and Vickie Weaver (*Charter members).

Gr. Greenville, North Carolina
Chapter #335, Region 11
Charter Date: August 4, 1990

The Gr. Greenville Chapter was chartered in August of 1990. We have established three annually-awarded scholarships. We hold two Block-Kids contests each year. We love sharing our helping hands in up-fitting a local project in need. The chapter held its 10th Anniversary Celebration on September 26, 2000. At the anniversary celebration, eight of the chartering members were honored for their 10 years of service and dedication to NAWIC's core purpose.

Tuscaloosa, Alabama
Chapter #336, Region 2
Charter Date: October 20, 1990

The Tuscaloosa Chapter was chartered in 1990 by founding member Jean Morris. The chapter has endowed a local scholarship fund for many years. As of 2004, the chapter has awarded scholarships to 28 students pursuing construction-related degrees. Years of conducting Block-Kids contests, Career Days and awarding scholarships have changed the local notion of women in construction from an oddity to a normality. This chapter also initiated the move to update the NAWIC logo. Even though this change was defeated in an Association-wide vote, the Tuscaloosa Chapter continues to appreciate NAWIC's openness to change in making NAWIC a relevant, respected construction association.

Temecula Valley, California
Chapter #338, Region 12
Charter Date: June 1, 1991

The Temecula Valley Chapter chartered in June of 1991, with more than 25 women from the Temecula Valley area in southwestern Riverside County in Southern California. The Pomona Valley Chapter was our chartering "mother," and with their guidance, our chapter hit the ground running. The chapter set out to make NAWIC history by offering a Truck Raffle in the fall of 1991. We sold a very limited number of tickets, which included a wonderful evening of dining and entertainment and one lucky winner walking away with a new Chevrolet truck. Temecula Valley set the stage for years of new, innovative ways to bring the message of NAWIC to the surrounding valley.

Northshore, Louisiana
Chapter #339, Region 5
Charter Date: June 8, 1991

The Northshore Chapter was chartered to encompass interested women outside of the New Orleans area. The chapter chartered with 33 members. Activities of the chapter have included presentations to school groups in an effort to interest young people in the construction industry; courses to members for professional improvement, particularly in the area of management; and also a networking service for persons hunting jobs in the field.

Central Missouri
Chapter #341, Region 6
Charter Date: August 10, 1991

The Central Missouri Chapter was chartered in 1991 to serve the Jefferson City – Columbia area. Over the years, we have had 12 Block-Kids contests, partnered with CSI for an annual golf tournament, held blueprint classes, participated in Career Days, worked with Habitat for Humanity, visited job sites and promoted construction in our area — all while having a great time. In 2004, we established the Central Missouri Chapter Scholarship Endowment in honor of Shirley Kidwell at LTSC. Our 15 to 20 members are doing their best to leave a positive impact on the construction industry in Central Missouri.

Manasota, Florida
Chapter #342, Region 3
Charter Date: August 17, 1991

Southeast Minnesota
Chapter #346, Region 13
Charter Date: March 26, 1993

Our chapter enjoys a variety of construction tours, as shown in this picture taken on the 27th story of Rochester's tallest building and largest apartment building. We had many tours of the new Mayo Clinic, a 20-story building. Riding the skipjack elevator is always fun! Founded in 1992, each year we host Block-Kids and CAD programs. Our annual fund raiser is a golf tournament. Monies from this tournament support our educational programs, including scholarships for young women at our local college. We are dedicated to giving back to our community, networking ideas and projects, and we enjoy spending time together at meetings and events.

Southern Maine
Chapter #347, Region 14
Charter Date: June 5, 1993

Maine's geographic size made it difficult for the only Maine Chapter to grow. So, members residing in Southern Maine were encouraged to form a new chapter. In June of 1993, Chapter #347 was off and running. Although we're a small chapter of only 11 members, we have contributed a lot to our community by hosting an Annual Spring Forum and Construction Rodeos, providing "guest chefs" at Portland's Ronald MacDonald House, providing labor to build a playground, volunteering with Habitat for Humanity, hosting a Design Drafting competition and setting up a scholarship fund. We continue to support NAWIC's philosophy by providing interesting agendas at our meetings.

The Magnolia Chapter, Mississippi
Chapter #352, Region 5
Charter Date: March 26, 1994

The Low Country of South Carolina
Chapter #354, Region 11
Charter Date: August 12, 1995

Space Coast Florida
Chapter #355, Region 3
Charter Date: October 15, 1996

Colorado Springs, Colorado
Chapter #356, Region 8
Charter Date: January 16, 1997

The Space Coast Chapter was chartered on October 5, 1996. It currently consists of 26 members who strive to emulate the core purpose of NAWIC, to enhance the success of women in the construction industry, through various community projects, educational and business-related programs. It is a very friendly, energetic and fun-loving group. The Space Coast Chapter is located in Brevard County Florida, which is known for its beautiful beaches and the Kennedy Space Center, home of NASA's Space Shuttle.

The Colorado Springs Chapter was chartered with the encouragement of the Denver, Colo., Chapter and Region 8 Director Pam Dullum. Until then, members were traveling to monthly meetings in Denver. The chapter chartered with 30 members. The chapter has become well-respected in the local construction industry, reaching out to the community in many ways. Chapter projects have included facilitating the construction of a safe house playground, Habitat for Humanity projects, constructing playhouses for CASA and coordinating the first Colorado Construction Career Days. Each project offers members the opportunity to learn more about construction and a time to stand back and see their hard work take shape.

Greater Madison, Wisconsin
Chapter #358, Region 13
Charter Date: October 26, 1997

The Greater Madison, Wis., Chapter is approximately eight years old. We participate in several community events, such as Block-Kids, Girl Scout Cookie Build, Dane County Paint-a-thon and a Scholarship Golf Outing. Our annual golf outing provides us with the resources to sponsor scholarships for women in the construction programs at local colleges.

Western Colorado
Chapter #359, Region 8
Charter Date: January 15, 2000

The chapter, chartered on January 15, 2000, was the first chapter chartered in the new millennium. We have hosted Annual Planning Conferences in 2001 and 2004. This year, we hosted our fifth annual gymkhana, our main fundraising event, and held our first-ever horse show. Block-Kids gets bigger and better for us every year. During WIC Week, we enjoy our signature equipment rodeo, obtain a proclamation from the mayor declaring it WIC Week locally and wear NAWIC attire throughout the week. In 2003, we established a scholarship fund to award to women in pursuit of a career in the industry.

Sugarloaf, Georgia
Chapter #360, Region 2
Charter Date: March 18, 2000

The Sugarloaf Chapter was chartered in March of 2000. In the four years since our chartering, the chapter has worked on building treehouses for disadvantaged children in the mountains of North Georgia. We have also renovated a recreation room for the men in Parkwood Rehab/Nursing Home. Eight of our members have passed the CIT course.

Sparks, Nevada
Chapter #361, Region 10
Charter Date: July 8, 2000

Pinnacles Chapter
Chapter #363, Region 10
Charter Date: October 7, 2000

Greater Gainesville, Florida
Chapter #364, Region 3
Charter Date: March 24, 2001

The chapter chartered in March 2001 with the help of Bobbie Cheh of the Volusia County Chapter. The chapter holds monthly meetings the second Tuesday of every month. It is involved with several community events including the Builders Association of North Central Florida's Parade of Homes, Habitat for Humanity and provides yearly assistance to a designated charitable organization. The chapter's most recent project involved renovations to a 12-year-old Habitat for Humanity home. Several workdays were held at the home where a new bathroom lavatory was installed, a screen porch was re-screened, the yard was cleaned of debris and landscaped, and a bedroom was painted.

Northwest Georgia
Chapter #365, Region 2
Charter Date: November 3, 2001

The Northwest Georgia Chapter was chartered November 3, 2001. Our chartering was an extension of the Atlanta, Ga., Chapter. Dorothy Gray, a long-time Atlanta member, was the chartering president, along with Tressie Colehour, vice president; Sharon Valery, CPA, treasurer; and Kristin House, secretary. We chartered with fifteen members. Over the years since our chartering, we have been involved in civic and community activities with our main focus being professional education.

Southwest Missouri
Chapter #366, Region 6
Charter Date: November 10, 2001

The Southwest Missouri chapter currently has 27 members and continues to grow. Each year, we give back to our community and women in construction by participating in activities with the Girl Scouts; repairing a play house at the Ronald McDonald House; creating "Comfort Kits" at the local Victim's Center; and hosting our first Block-Kids in January of 2004 and continued again in 2005. Each year, we award two women with the "Outstanding Woman in Construction" awards. Our biggest event is the annual A-Z Seminar in which we bring in speakers from the community to talk about issues facing us in the industry.

Bluegrass, Kentucky
Chapter #367, Region 4
Charter Date: December 1, 2001

And so it began, a small gathering of heartbroken, stunned yet determined women, met in Lexington, Ky., on September 13, 2001, two days after our country had been attacked. Cincinnati and Louisville members sponsored our new chapter in December 2001. Born amid chaos and NAWIC perseverance, we have grown from 6 to 55. Using chapter and community resources, our outstanding speakers have been educational and motivational. Chapter members are active in regional and national events. We participate in at least three community service projects each year. We are the Bluegrass Chapter, and we have big plans for the future!

Lake/McHenry County of Illinois
Chapter #368, Region 13
Charter Date: January 19, 2002

The Lake/McHenry Chapter of Region 13 was chartered on January 19, 2002. The sponsoring chapter was the O'Hare Suburban Chapter. Charter members consisted of seventeen women from all phases of the construction industry.

Blue Ridge, Virginia
Chapter #369, Region 11
Charter Date: June 21, 2002

This chapter was formed on June 21, 2002, with 25 chartering members who had an idea they could be more productive, more successful and more united. National President Linda Litle and Region 11 Director Carol Chapman, along with the support of so many others from the region, attended our chartering banquet. We hit the ground running, and in only two years, we continually fulfill the NAWIC core purpose, making significant contributions to the community while advancing individually. We proudly boast seven CIT's and five CDS's, and we're just getting started! We look forward to the next 50 years.

South Atlanta Alliance, Georgia
Chapter #370, Region 2
Charter Date: August 24, 2002

Mobile Bay Area, Alabama
Chapter #371, Region 2
Charter Date: December 7, 2002

"Well, I have to run for now. I have to get everything ready for tonight," said Pat Bruce. "So you have a hot date tonight?" I asked. "Oh no, I have a NAWIC Field Trip," she replied. "What's NAWIC?" I asked. That is how the Mobile Bay Area Chapter #371 came into being. It took more than a year to get 17 members to charter our chapter on December 7, 2003, and we have been growing ever since. Of the original charter members, we have six still active, and we are undertaking the daunting task of hosting our first Region 2 Forum this April. Happy 50th NAWIC!!!!

Phoenix East Valley, Arizona
Chapter #373, Region 8
Charter Date: June 29, 2003

Greater Jacksonville, Florida
Chapter #372, Region 3
Charter Date: January 25, 2003

The Florida beaches and fantastic climate are two reasons people and companies are attracted to Jacksonville; this includes NAWIC. In January 2003, the chapter began. Since chartering, we have been involved with many activities from WIC Week Blood Drives to AIA CANstructure. We have worked hard to get our chapter off and running. There are many great memories NAWIC cultivates, but the way we interact together is indescribable. The friendships formed will stay with each and every one of us for years to come. As Jacksonville's construction industry grows, so does our chapter.

*NAWIC's 50th Anniversary flag is proudly
displayed outside the NAWIC office.*

Index

NATIONAL ASSOCIATION OF
WOMEN IN CONSTRUCTION
NAWIC